THE INDIE WRITER'S ENCYCLOPEDIA

All the Terms You Need to Know to Be a Successful Writer

M.L. RONN

Contents

To my former self,

Who desperately needed this book

Introduction

Here's what you're going to learn in this book: every term you need to know to work and prosper as an indie writer, along with practical examples of how to apply an understanding of those terms to your career.

When I started my journey as an author, I was astounded by the mountain of information I had to learn.

It wasn't just about writing a book; I had to learn business, marketing, cover design, legal terms, and so much more.

And I'll admit...I was an English major in college, and nothing other than writing came naturally to me.

This was back in 2014.

Today, I look at the publishing industry and see so much more complexity than when I started.

There's so much to learn, and for a technical-minded person like me, that's exciting.

But not everyone is me. Some people just want to know the basics and learn as they go. That's not always easy in this industry.

Who I Am and Why I Wrote This Book

At the time of this writing, I've written over 40 books, available in ebook, paperback, and audio.

I run a YouTube channel called Author Level Up where I publish weekly videos with advice for writers. I've created over 200 helpful videos for writers wanting to take their writing to the next level. Right now, the channel has tens of thousands of subscribers and it's an amazing community of dedicated writers. Some of my most popular videos are ones in which I explain terms and concepts.

I'm also the United States ambassador for The Alliance of Independent Authors (ALLi for short), a nonprofit organization whose mission is ethics and excellence in self-publishing and to help self-published authors be the creative directors of their careers. I've hosted two podcasts for self-publishing beginners: *The Beginner's Self-Publishing Salon* and the *AskALLi Member Q&A Podcast*, in which I, alongside ALLi Director Orna Ross, answer common and advanced self-publishing questions, things like "How should I outline my book?", "What is copyright and why do I need it?", and "What is a reversion-of-rights clause and should I sign a contract with that in it?" I've answered over 200 self-publishing questions, and when you get that many questions, you start to see some commonalities.

I get a fair number of questions every day on my YouTube channel, podcasts, and email inbox from writers wanting to know something about virtually every aspect of self-publishing. As a result, I've had to sharpen my knowledge of many different areas of the industry. I found myself thinking one day, "Wouldn't it have been nice if there were a dictionary or encyclopedia for writers to reference whenever they had a question about a publishing term?"

So I created this book. It's a hybrid between a dictionary and an encyclopedia, with over 300 terms to help you grasp the basic concepts of writing and non-writing frameworks that every working indie author needs to know. They include writing, business, legal, and marketing terms that you'll encounter regularly.

These terms are referenced on writing blogs, writing podcasts, writing books, and everyday conversations between writers at conferences. Knowing them will help you carry the conversation instead of stopping to ask, "Wait, what's offset printing again?"

Where it makes sense, the book also includes detailed explanations of the terms using examples specifically for authors. No more Googling terms and trying to figure out how they apply to authors. The book also includes internal references and appendices to help you continue the learning after you've finished with this book.

This book is several years' worth of writing education in one book. I wish I'd had it when I started writing. Keep it as a reference for yourself any time you need a refresher on something.

Is it perfect? No. The terms I define here are based on my own experience both as a writer who's had to experience them in some shape or form, and as a consultant helping other writers who have needed help with a certain situation.

Are there more terms that I could have included? Yes, and with your feedback, maybe I can incorporate them into the next edition.

In the meantime, sit back and enjoy. I hope you'll find this book as entertaining as I did writing it.

— M.L. Ronn
April 20, 2019
Des Moines, Iowa

A

About Page

1. The webpage on an author's site that describes who they are

Also known as a Bio Page.

After the homepage, the about page is typically the most visited page on any website. Common elements of about pages include brief biographies of the author, a personal message from the author, a manifesto, a mailing list sign-up, a favorite book list, photographs of the author, or embedded audio or video recorded by the author.

See *Endnotes*.

Acknowledgments

1. Front or back matter element where the author expresses gratitude for the people who helped produce the book

Acknowledgments (also spelled as "acknowledgements") can appear in the front or back matter of a book. Traditionally, they appear in the front matter after the preface but before the introduction or prologue of the book. They may also appear in the back matter. However, a more recent trend is to incorporate acknowledgments credits into other front or back matter pages, such as the copyright page, preface, or the author's note. In self-published ebooks, it is also a commonly-accepted practice to place the acknowledgments in the back of the book in order to make the book's retail sample contain more of the book and less front matter.

See Author's Note, Back Matter, Copyright Page, Front Matter, and Preface.

See also Appendix A: Front and Back Matter.

Acquisitions Board

1. At a traditional publisher, a group of people who make decisions about what books to acquire for publication

See *Traditional Publisher*.

Active Income

1. Income derived from activities that require ongoing effort

Active income activities include hand-selling books at conventions, author signings, and social media promotions, to name a few. Generally, in order to make money from these activities, you have to do them regularly and often.

See *Income Stream* and *Passive Income*.

Advance

1. A sum of money paid to an author upon signing a publishing contract that serves as a payment against future royalties

If an author receives a $1000 advance from a publisher, the book will have to earn the publisher $1000 before the author will see any additional royalties. For this reason, it is best to think of an advance as an advance against future royalties rather than a signing bonus.

See *Royalty*.

Advance Print Run

1. Printing of advanced review copies of a book printed before the book's official release date, usually for publicity purposes

See *Advanced Review Copy (ARC)*.

Advanced Reader Copy (ARC)

1. A pre-publication copy of an author's book sent to
   readers to secure early reviews, feedback, and buzz

See *Review* and *Street Team*.

Affiliate Marketing

1. Revenue-sharing arrangement where individuals
   ("affiliates") are paid commissions for selling and
   promoting the products and services of other
   businesses

The most popular and internationally-recognized affiliate
program in the world is Amazon Associates. Nearly anyone can
sign up to be an Amazon Associate, and they can include
Amazon affiliate links on their website—if someone clicks on
an affiliate link and buys anything on Amazon, the associate
receives a small commission because the theory is that they
helped create a sale where one wouldn't have existed otherwise.

While Amazon is the most easily understood example of
affiliate marketing, many entrepreneurs pay affiliate commissions for their products, services, and online courses, usually
offering affiliates free copies in exchange for a review. The affiliate then makes commissions on any future sales they refer.

Affiliate marketing can sometimes involve ethical and legal perils. Some countries like the United States legally require affiliates to disclose any affiliate links and/or whether they received a product for free to avoid misleading customers.

While affiliate income may not be as lucrative for books, writers can still make affiliate income by promoting books, products, and services that they use or enjoy to their audiences.

See *Cash Flow*, *Content Marketing*, *Income Stream*, *Passive Income*.

Agency Clause

1. Section in a publishing contract that allows a literary agent to collect royalties from the publisher, deduct commissions, exercise rights of refusal, place liens on future books written by the author, and potentially claim copyright ownership in an author's work(s)

Michael's opinion: When you're dealing with an honest and reputable literary agency, the agency clause is how the literary agent asserts legal and financial acknowledgment for their contribution to the publishing process. However, in many cases, the agency clause is an extremely dubious clause that can cripple an author's career and copyrights in devastating ways. If you ever find yourself looking at one, consult an intellectual property attorney immediately.

.   .   .

See *Literary Agent*.

See also *Appendix B: Resources for More Learning* for additional resources to help you assess a publishing contract.

Agency Pricing Model

1. Sales model where the book publisher sets the price of the book and the retailer takes a commission for each sale

Let's say that an author self-publishes a book on Amazon. For every sale, the author receives 70% of the sale and Amazon receives 30%. That is how agency pricing works, and it is usually the sales model used for ebooks and digital products sold on online retailers such as Amazon and Apple. Agency pricing differs from wholesale pricing in that the retailer cannot discount the price of the book.

See *Wholesale Pricing*.

Alignment

1. The arrangement of text on the page, generally in relation to the left margin

See *Justification* and *Margin*.

Alpha Reader

1. An early reader who reads an author's work before publication, usually before the author begins self-editing

Also known as a first reader. An alpha reader differs from a beta reader in that they are someone the author trusts who reads the unpolished manuscript and offers feedback on if the story works. Whereas an author can enlist any number of beta readers, an author typically only enlists one or two alpha readers.

See *Advanced Reader Copy*, *Beta Reader*, *Minimum Viable Product*, and *Sensitivity Reader*.

Also Bought

1. Section on an Amazon product page that displays items that other customers have also purchased

Amazon Also Boughts are arguably one of the most powerful features to help authors sell more books. When filled with similar books in the genre, they are one way that readers can discover books. When not filled with similar books however, they can hurt a book's discoverability.

.   .   .

See *Appendix B: Resources for More Learning* for resources on understanding the Amazon Algorithms.

Alt Tag

1. Alternate text for an image that displays in an Internet browser

Also known as an alt description or alt text.

Alt tags are metadata for images that explain what is in the image if and when the image does not load. They are useful for the visually impaired or for people who may be using text-only browsers. Utilizing alt tags is universally considered a must for any website not just because they improve the user experience for the visually impaired, but because they also help with Search Engine Optimization (SEO). Search engines read and index images based on what alt tags say.

Amazon Standard Identification Number (ASIN)

1. A unique alphanumeric number assigned to every product sold on Amazon

Unlike the International Standard Book Number (ISBN), which can be used anywhere, an ASIN is only found on Amazon. It is how Amazon identifies their products. Books that have ISBNs also have ASINs.

· · ·

See *International Standard Book Number*.

Antagonist

1. The villain of a story and the driving force against
   the protagonist

Commonly confused with *Antihero*.

See *Protagonist*.

Anthology

1. A collection of themed short stories, novellas, or
   poems curated by an editor

See *Box Set*.

Anti-climactic

1. A term that expresses disappointment in how events
   unfold after a certain part in a story, usually the
   final battle

Anti-climactic is a term often used by readers and movie watchers to describe an ending of a novel or movie. For example, it could mean there was a lot of hype leading up to the final battle, but either the final battle was disappointing and didn't deliver, or the story ended so quickly after the final battle that it wasn't satisfying.

See *Climax*, *Denouement*, *Final Battle*, and *Freytag's Pyramid*.

Appendix

1. Supplemental material at the end of a book that provides additional information not covered in the book

Appendices are most commonly used in nonfiction to delve deeper into topics that the author wasn't able to explore in the body of the book. They could include sources for additional reading, links to articles or videos, or graphs and charts.

See *Glossary*.

See also *Appendix A: Front and Back Matter*.

Artificial Intelligence (AI)

1. The ability of computer systems to perform tasks

normally performed by humans, but faster and
more accurately
2. A computer system or algorithm

See *Disintermediation.*

Assisted Self-Publisher

1. A company that provides formatting, publishing,
marketing and promotion services to self-published
authors

See *Hybrid Publisher* and *Vanity Publisher.*

Audiobook

1. A digital audio, CD, or an audiocassette edition of
a book read by a narrator

Audiobooks began as cassette tapes and CDs, and while CDs
are still prevalent today, digital audiobooks have been growing
in popularity because of their convenience. People like them
because of the emergence of smartphone apps that allow them
to listen to books while they are driving, doing chores, exercis-
ing, etc.

While expensive to produce, the audiobook format has

become an extremely lucrative investment for authors who can afford to produce their books in the format, and there are many audiobook publishers who only publish books in audio and make a lot of money doing it.

The famous novel *The Martian* by Andy Weir began its life as a self-published ebook that was picked up by Podium Publishing, a reputable audiobook publisher. The audiobook played a major part in launching the book into the public consciousness, leading to a six-figure print deal, a movie, and much more. Weir's success paved the way for self-published authors to attract major attention in the audiobook market.

Also stylized as abook, compared to ebooks and pbooks.

See *Narrator*.

Authorpreneur

1. An author who treats his/her writing like a business, and who aims to (or does) make a living selling books and from associated business activities

See *Independent (Indie) Publisher*, *Self-Publishing*, and *Virtual Assistant*.

Author's Note

1. Back matter element where the author talks about why they wrote the book or what inspired it.

Also known as a postscript.

See *Acknowledgments, Back Matter, Conclusion, Foreword, Introduction,* and *Preface.*

See also *Appendix A: Front and Back Matter.*

Autoresponder

1. Sequence of automated emails sent to mailing list subscribers that educate them on a topic
2. An automatic email that lets email senders know that you are unable to respond to email (known as a "vacation responder" or "out of office reply"); popular in email clients

For definition #1, an autoresponder is also known as a follow-up. Autoresponders are an effective email marketing technique. Their power lies in their automation and the ability to set rules. Many authors time autoresponders to send every few days for a set period of time to help new mailing list subscribers learn more about the author and the books they write. They can even create conditional autoresponders that go to a subscriber if they take a certain action, like clicking on a specific link in an email. When written authentically, they help keep readers "warm" until an author has a new book to share.

For definition #2, just know that some people may use the word autoresponder to refer to an out of office email, particularly in the corporate world.

. . .

See *Campaign*, *Mailing List*, and *Segmentation*.

B

Backlist

1. The body of work published prior to an author's newest release

Also known as inventory.

See *Frontlist*.

Back Matter

1. Elements of a book that appear immediately after the body

Author's notes, appendices, bibliographies, author biographies, and other books by the author are common examples of back matter.

See *Front Matter*.

See also *Appendix A: Front and Back Matter*.

Beta Reader

1. An early reader who reads an author's work before publication, usually after the author has finished self-editing

See *Advanced Reader Copy*, *Alpha Reader*, and *Sensitivity Reader*.

Bibliography

1. In fiction, a list of books the author has written
2. In nonfiction, back matter element that contains a list of books referred to in the body, compiled for further reading

See *Back Matter* and *Endnotes*.
See *Appendix A: Front and Back Matter*.

"Big Five" Publishers

1. The largest five traditional trade publishers in the United States: Hachette, HarperCollins, Macmillan, Penguin Random House, and Simon & Schuster

Typically, the only way to get published by one of the Big Five is to have a literary agent.

See *Imprint, Trade Publishing* and *Traditional Publisher*.

Binding

1. The method in which the pages of a book are held together

Books can be bound in a number of different ways. For example, saddle-stitching is used for smaller books where a wire or a series of staple holds the pages together, as is done with many poetry chapbooks. Perfect bound books have pages that are glued to the spine with a strong but flexible glue, as is done with many trade paperbacks. Hardcover or case bound books use a combination of glue and stitching to bind the pages to the spine. And of course, there is spiral binding, which is used for standard notebooks. These are just a few of the many different binding types.

See *Casewrap, Perfect Bound*, and *Saddle-Stitching*.

Bleed

1. The area outside where the book page will be cut

Bleeds come into play when you have text or images that are potentially larger than the trim size of your book. Therefore, you have to scale your content down in order to keep everything in the safe, printable areas.

If you don't do your own formatting and cover design, then this won't be important to you. But if you do either of these, it's important to pay close attention to the bleed, because if you don't, your book will look unprofessional and your content will be clipped when printed. Print on-demand services such as KDP Print and Ingram Spark provide templates and specific instructions to help you avoid issues with the bleed.

See *Margin*.

Blockchain

1. A digital record of cryptocurrency transactions that cannot be altered

For all the buzz around cryptocurrencies, perhaps the most important piece of the technology for authors is the blockchain.

The blockchain removes intermediaries and provides an indisputable trail of transactions and ownership, which has potentially transformative impacts to royalties, author payments, and copyright licensing and ownership for writers.

See *Cryptocurrency, Disintermediation*, and *Smart Contract*.

Blog

1. A regularly updated website or series of webpages around a theme or group of topics, written in a conversational style by one or multiple writers, easily shared on social media

Originally known as a weblog (archaic).

See *Podcast* and *Vlog*.

Blurb

1. A short testimonial by an author or a reader that praises a book
2. Another term for a book description (incorrect)

While the term "blurb" is often substituted for a "book description" in everyday conversation, that usage is not technically correct. Merriam-Webster defines "blurb" as "a short publicity notice (as on a book jacket)."

A blurb can appear on the front or back cover of a book, in the front or back matter, on a book's product page, or in any other place where the author is trying to promote their book.

Also known as an endorsement quote.

.   .   .

See *Back Matter*, *Book Description*, and *Front Matter*.

See also *Appendix A: Front and Back Matter*.

Body

1. The main story or text of a book, not including the front or back matter

Boilerplate Language

1. Standardized, non-negotiable language in a publishing contract that is offered equally to all of the publisher's authors

Publishers (and businesses and attorneys in general) use boilerplate language to standardize their business dealings. With the sheer volume of contracts they offer each year, they benefit from the efficiency and uniformity that boilerplate language provides. However, boilerplate language may often run counter to an author's interests.

See *Terms of Service*.

See also *Appendix D: Copyright.*

Book Blog

1. A blog run by someone who primarily publishes
   book reviews (who is known as a book blogger)

Book bloggers are usually book enthusiasts who publish their
blog in their free time. Few are able to go full-time with the
effort, so as a result, they tend to be backlogged with author
requests for reviews, and the best way to get book blogger
reviews is to query as many (relevant) book bloggers as possible.
It's a numbers game.

See *Review* and *Vlog*.

Book Description

1. A summary or synopsis of a book that entices
   readers to buy

A modern book description consists of three parts: a headline
that grabs the reader's attention, the description itself, and a
call-to-action or a thought-provoking final line that convinces
the reader to buy. A book description may also contain blurbs,
and on product pages, it may include creative elements such as
a brief Q&A with the author.

See *Blurb*.

Book Fair

1. Exhibition for publishers, authors, and booksellers, usually in a convention center (such as the London Book Fair)

In this context, a book fair is where publishers, authors, and booksellers network and form connections. New technologies and initiatives are displayed, and it's not uncommon for publishers to find authors to sign.

Book Industry Standards and Communications (BISAC)

1. A universal metadata classification system used by bookstores and online retailers to organize books

BISAC codes were developed by the Book Industry Study Group (BISG), a trade organization with the goal to help standardize the transfer of book metadata across the industry. They ensure that bookstores and publishers are speaking the same language when they classify books for sale.

Any given BISAC code consists of two parts: an alphanumeric code and a genre descriptor.

For example, as explained on the BISG website, a travel book that takes place in the southern United States would have the alphanumeric code TRV025070 and the genre descriptor TRAVEL / United States / South / General. The most important part of any code is the descriptor, because the descriptors are the categories that writers select when they upload their books to book retailers. Almost all retailers use the BISAC codes to organize their books for readers to browse. Some, like Amazon, use the BISAC codes as a starting point and have additional categories that authors can use.

See *Category* and *Metadata*.

Book Promotion "Promo" Site

1. A website that has amassed a mailing list of hundreds of thousands of targeted readers (usually segmented by genre or subgenre), and that charge authors a fee to promote books to those readers

"Ad stacking" is the process of chaining together ads at multiple promo sites in order to improve exposure for a book, usually at launch.

See *Marketing* and *Promotion*.

Book Proposal

1. A pitch document that an author creates to pitch an idea for a nonfiction book to an agent publisher

The book proposal is used by publishers to gauge if an idea is worth publishing and if there is a market for it.

. . .

See *Query Letter*.

For fiction, see *Book Synopsis*.

Book Retailer

1. A business that sells physical books, ebooks, or
   audiobooks

A "brick and mortar" retailer refers to a retailer whose primary
presence is physical books (i.e. an independent bookstore). A
"click and mortar" retailer has both a physical and online presence, like Barnes & Noble in the United States or Waterstones
in the United Kingdom. And of course there are purely online
retailers as well.

See *Distributor*, *Ebook Aggregator*, and *Independent Bookstore*.

Book Sample

1. The first few pages of a book or the first few
   minutes of an audiobook that online readers can
   browse at a book retailer to determine whether they
   should buy

Book Synopsis

1. A summary of a novel's plot for a prospective agent or publisher so they can see what happens in the story and if the novel is worth publishing

For fiction, an author writes a novel and then pitches it to publishers. For nonfiction, the author typically pitches the idea first, then continues writing if the publisher is interested.

For fiction, see *Query Letter*.

For nonfiction, see *Book Proposal*.

Book Trailer

1. Short video advertising a book, usually with graphics, music, and/or actors

Boutique Agency

1. A literary agency that is small in size and/or highly specialized

The term is used by literary agents to differentiate themselves from bigger agencies. A boutique agency may specialize in representing Young Adult writers, for example.

See *Literary Agent*.

Box Set

1. A compilation of several novels, novellas, or short stories by different authors, usually created for the purpose of cross-promoting similar authors to a target audience; may be short-term or long-term

Indie authors didn't create the box set, but they certainly reinvented it. The technique is most commonly used by indie authors to create exposure for their books. Unlike an anthology, a box set does not usually have an editor, but there may be a foreword by a famous author, and the existence of more popular authors is almost always used to draw readers to help them discover lesser-known authors in the collection.

See *Anthology*, *Bundling*, and *Cross-Promotion*.

Bundling

1. The act of selling different books or items together as a package

See *Box Set, Cross-Sell,* and *Upsell.*

Buyer Persona

1. A fictional representation of an author's target reader, their demographics, buying behaviors, and preferences based on real data

Also known as a customer avatar or reader persona.

Buyer personas are frequently used by businesses to get into the heads of their customers so they can market to them better. By creating an ideal customer profile, they can design products with the buyer persona in mind.

C

Call to Action (CTA)

1. A compelling argument to get a customer to do something that will solve a problem they have, such as buying a product

Also known as a sales handle.

See *Conversion*, *Mailing List*, and *Squeeze Page*.

Campaign

1. A one-time newsletter sent to an online mailing list
2. A limited time in which an ad is served to an audience ("ad campaign")

Definition #1 (a one-time newsletter) is also known as a broadcast or newsletter. The terminology depends on the email provider.

See *Autoresponder* and *Mailing List*.

Casewrap

1. Style of hardcover book where the cover image is

printed on the case (cover)

Because the cover image is printed directly on the case of the book, casewrap hardcovers look similar to trade paperbacks except that they have a hardcover. Casewrap hardcovers are more cost-effective to print than traditional hardcover dust jackets.

See *Binding* and *Dust Jacket*.

Cash Flow

1. The flow of money in and out of a business, and an important indicator of its vitality

See *Active Income*, *Income Stream*, and *Passive Income*.

Category

1. Division in an online retailer where a book is located

Usually, category is synonymous with genre, but they are not always the same. For example, a poetry book written by Maya Angelou would be located in the poetry category at whatever online retailer you buy it. But the book would also be placed into subcategories based on what is available under the BISAC system. In Maya Angelou's case, poetry can be categorized by the ethnicity, gender, or the nationality of the author, so the category listing for an ebook written by her might look like this: Poetry / American / African-American or Poetry / Women.

On almost all online retailers, bestseller lists are organized by categories.

See *Book Industry Standards and Communications (BISAC)* and *Metadata*.

Cease & Desist

1. A court-enforceable order that seeks to stop a person from engaging in a particular activity, with the threat of legal action if the person does not

Authors can receive a cease & desist order (abbreviated as C&D) for any number of reasons. For example, if an author is using someone else's trademark on their book cover, the owner of the trademark can issue a cease & desist to prevent further sales of the book with the trademark on the cover.

If an author is making disparaging comments about another author online, the disparaged author can issue a cease & desist order to ask the author to stop with a warning that further comments will lead to a lawsuit.

Chapbook

1. A small, limited run booklet, usually containing

poetry

See *Saddle-Stitching*.

Chapter

1. The main unit of division in a story, with a number or title

How many chapters should be in a book? The answer is that it depends on the author and the genre! Some novels have only a few, and others have well over 100. There's no steadfast rule to how many chapters your book should have.

See *Novel*.

Character Sketch

1. A write-up of a character's demographics, background, and other details to help a writer get familiar enough with the character to write a story

Some writers find character sketches valuable to help them get into their characters' heads. It is usually done in conjunction with outlining, but it is not a required part of the writing process.

. . .

See *Freewriting* and *Outlining*.

Chicago Manual of Style

1. Standardized style guide used by authors, editors, and publishers

The Chicago Manual of Style is the gold standard of style guides in journalism and publishing, and it is the one reputable editors use. It offers guidance on comma usage, manuscript formatting, and source citation, among many things. Academics use the Modern Language Association (MLA) or the American Psychological Association (APA) style guides.

See *Editing* and *Editor*.

Chronology

1. Front or back matter element with a timeline of events in or leading up to a book

See *Front Matter* and *Back Matter*.

See also *Appendix A: Front and Back Matter*.

Click Rate

1. An email marketing statistic that measures the percentage of people who click a link in any given newsletter or autoresponder
2. In advertising, the percentage of people who click an ad, most commonly known as a click-through rate

The click rate is important because it measures how well your email copy entices your readers to take action. You want your readers to open AND click on the links in your emails.

A high click rate indicates that readers are reading your emails to the end and clicking through to wherever you want them to go (such as the product page of a new book). A low click rate indicates weak copy, and you may need to adjust your messaging, sentence length, paragraph pacing, and even your call-to-action in order to improve it.

See *Conversion*, *Mailing List*, and *Open Rate*.

Climax

1. The most exciting or intense part of a story; often the final battle

See *Anti-climactic*, *Final Battle*, and *Freytag's Pyramid*.

Cold Open

1. In film and television, a narrative technique where a film or show opens suddenly in the middle of the story before the title credits appear (if they appear at all)
2. In fiction, when a story or chapter begins in the middle of action without first introducing the characters or the stakes

In television, famous examples of shows that use cold opens are *The Office* and the **HBO** television series *The Wire*.

In fiction, the cold open is an advanced narrative technique. Generally, an author starts a story or chapter by establishing the setting, why the character is there, and what the stakes are before the events in the story proper begin. The cold open forgoes that and puts the reader *in media res* to hook them on the action, and the author sets the stakes and does a proper introduction of the character and setting shortly after.

See *In Media Res*.

See also *Appendix B: Resources for More Learning*.

Collaboration

1. The act of one or more authors writing a book together
2. The act of one or more authors working together to

cross-promote each other's books

For definition #2, an example of collaboration would be two authors who agree to promote the other's book in their monthly newsletter. This exposes both author's audiences to the books and drives sales. For the most effective results, collaboration is best done by authors in the same genre and subgenre.

See *Cross-Promotion.*

Collaborative Consumption

1. An economic model based on the sharing, swapping, or renting of services

Also known as the "sharing economy" and the "gig economy." AirBnB, Uber, and Fiverr are examples of companies that operate with the collaborative consumption model.

See *Active Income* and *Freelancing.*

Colon

1. A punctuation mark used to precede lists, explanations, or an expansion of an idea that comes before it

The colon is a powerful punctuation mark for one reason: it tells the reader to pay attention because something important is about to follow (see what I did there?)

In nonfiction, colons are everywhere: authors use them to list ideas (like I'm doing right now), expand on ideas, and as a way to get the reader's attention.

In fiction, there's one reason that you don't see them often: writers don't think they're important.

Hopefully, in just three sentences, you can see the power of the colon and how effective it can be as a writing tool.

See *Semi-Colon*.

Colophon

1. Front or back matter element that provides information about the book such as the fonts, the publisher, and where it was printed

Pronounced "Kuh-LA-fin".

A colophon is a mark of artistry. It started in ancient times as a way for scribes to put a personal mark on a manuscript. In modern times, they are used by publishers to detail how the book was printed. You'll often see information about the publisher, the type of paper the book was printed on, the fonts used, the printing method, etc.

Historically, the most common place for a colophon was in the back matter, on the very last page of the book, but in modern books you can find them at the front as well. However, most modern books have forgone the colophon altogether, instead incorporating the most important elements of it into the copyright page it needed.

See *Back Matter*, *Copyright Page*, and *Front Matter*.

See also *Appendix A: Front and Back Matter*.

Comma

1. A punctuation mark that denotes a pause between parts of a sentence

The comma is the most difficult punctuation mark to get right, and it's the most controversial in editing.

See *Serial Comma*.

Conclusion

1. In nonfiction, a back matter element where the author sums up final ideas and arguments

See *Author's Note*, and *Back Matter*.

. . .

See also *Appendix A: Front and Back Matter.*

Conversion

1. In formatting and publishing, the act of transforming an ebook from one format into another (such as ePUB to MOBI)
2. In marketing, the transformation of a prospective customer into a buying customer

See *Call to Action, Click Rate, Impressions, Pop-Up, Sales Funnel, Split Test,* and *Mailing List.*

Content Marketing

1. A style of marketing where marketers promote products via content such as blogs, podcasts, and online video, and where the product itself is not the sole focus of the content, but an important element

In a digital age where consumers are bombarded with ads, more brands have turned to content marketing because the content is a softer pitch, it's shareable, and it can often stand on its own.

In 2017, the U.S. fast food chain KFC released a romance novel called *Tender Wings of Desire* with its iconic Colonel Sanders as the lead. KFC released the book in honor of Mother's Day, a historically high sales day for the franchise. The book went viral, and according to many, the book was actually pretty decent. This is content marketing at its finest.

A more common example of content marketing is a lawn care blogger talking about their weekly lawn care, and how they use a certain organic fertilizer because of how the fertilizer aligns with their strategy of not using too many chemicals on the lawn. The fertilizer discussion is just one part of the overall theme of the video.

See *Affiliate Marketing, Influencer, Microinfluencer* and *Native Content*.

Contest

1. A competition where authors submit novels, poems, or short stories to a judge or pool of judges in hopes of winning a literary award or prize; it may or may not require a fee

Co-op Advertising

1. Style of advertising where the cost is shared between different companies; most cost-effective for smaller companies with smaller advertising budgets

Copy

1. In advertising, the written words in an advertisement
2. In publishing, the text of a book

Copyediting

1. Type of editing in which an editor reviews a manuscript line-by-line to correct errors and bring it into accordance with a style guide

Also known as line editing.

See *Developmental Editing*, *Editing*, *Editor*, and *Proofreading*.

Copyright

1. In publishing, the exclusive right of an author to print, publish, sell, or license a literary work for profit

Under the Berne Convention Agreement, many countries uniformly recognize that copyright lasts for the author's life plus 70 years.

Copyright doesn't protect words or ideas, but instead the way they are expressed.

See *Copyright Notice*, *Copyright Page*, *Creative Commons*, *Digital Rights Management*, *Fair Use*, *Infringement*, *Intellectual Property*, *Piracy*, *Public Domain*, *Royalty-Free*, *Stock Content*, *Trademark*, *Trade Dress*, and *Work for Hire*.

· · ·

See also *Appendix D: Copyright*.

Copyright Notice

1. A written declaration of ownership of a copyright, printed on the copyright page

The example of this book's copyright notice is Copyright @ 2019 M.L. Ronn.

See *Copyright*.

Copyright Page

1. Front matter element that contains the copyright notice

See *Acknowledgments*, *Colophon*, and *Copyright Notice*.

Copywriting

1. In marketing and advertising, the act of writing advertisements that convinces a person to take a particular action

Copywriting is a completely different skill than writing a book.

Generally, authors write books to entertain or educate. Copywriters write to persuade people to buy, sign up for a mailing list, donate money, or some other action that is necessary for a business to make money. Because it is a different skill, it requires a different mindset.

See *Appendix D: Copyright.*

Cover

1. Most commonly, the image printed on the front of the book with the author name, book title, and graphics that represent the contents of the book; may also refer to the back of the book
2. The physical front, back, and spine of a book

See *Typography*.

Cover Spread

1. The entire cover of a physical book, from the front, including the spine, to the back

Cozy Mystery

1. A subgenre of mystery in which an amateur detective solves a murder, usually in a small town

See *Mystery.*

See also Appendix C: Fiction Genres.

Creative Commons

1. A public copyright licensing system that determines how and when a work can be shared

Creative Commons evolved as a way for content creators to share and protect their copyrighted work while also allowing and encouraging remixing and creative freedom.

Any content creator can assign a Creative Commons license to their work that dictates what can be done with the work—for example, the creator can release the work into the public domain or mandate that the work is shareable, but only if the original creator is attributed. Or, the creator may not allow anyone to share or remix the work at all without written permission.

Where authors frequently run into Creative Commons is in finding images for their blog or social media. Photos are copyrighted and many photographers will seek to enforce their copyrights if they are not respected, which can result in legal troubles for an author. It is very important to look for a Creative Commons license on any image you want to use for any purpose. When in doubt, don't share or remix any image that you do not have permission to. The safest option of all is to purchase royalty-free images, but even then, sometimes that's not a complete guarantee.

An answer to a common question: generally, it is okay to share content posted on a social media network (like a viral video) because the creator's original intent was that the work be shared. This type of content is usually not marked with a Creative Commons license.

See *Copyright*, *Fair Use*, *Public Domain*, *Stock Content*, and *Royalty-Free*.

Cross-Promotion

1. The act of two or more authors promoting the other's work

See *Box Set* and *Collaboration*.

Cross-Sell

1. The act of an author selling other products to a reader either before, at, or after the point of sale

A classic example of cross-selling is a "Other Books by the Author" page in the back matter of a book.

Cross-selling can also involve products other than books. For example, if the author sells t-shirts or other merchandise and promotes those to readers, that's also cross-selling.

. . .

See *Bundling* and *Upsell*.

Crowdfunding

1. The act of raising money from an audience in order to fund a project
2. The act of patronage from fans (such as through Patreon)

Crowdfunding has grown in popularity in recent years as creators use the power of their audience. For example, if an author wanted to fund the creation of a graphic novel edition of their book, they may ask that their audience make donations to a Kickstarter campaign to help pay for it. In exchange for making a donation, the author may give readers bonuses such as free copies of the work, access to behind-the-scenes footage, and unused art.

Michael's opinion only: I don't recommend crowd-funding the creation of a book (ebook or paperback), absent extreme extenuating circumstances. Readers expect you to pay for those expenses and in general are reluctant to pay for the production of a book that the author should have paid for in the first place. Hardcovers are fair game, though, as are any other formats, such as a graphic novel or a fan film, for example. These types of format are more difficult and more expensive to produce, and they're rarer to see among the ranks of self-published works.

See *Crowdsourcing*.

Crowdsourcing

1. The act of leveraging an audience for help in creating a project, such as an app

Crowdsourcing differs from crowdfunding. With crowdfunding, you're asking for money. With crowdsourcing, you're asking for services and time.

Wikipedia is the most famous example of crowdsourcing of all time. Anyone can add or edit articles. Wikipedia enlists the help of volunteer editors who police the content and make sure that it adheres to strict guidelines.

Another example of crowdsourcing is an app that a developer creates using programming help, beta testing, and input from an entire community of people who have a vested interest in using the app.

See *Crowdfunding*.

Cyberpunk

1. Science fiction subgenre, usually in a futuristic or alternative world where a certain resource is limited, a government or organization controls access to that resource, and a group of people fight against that power

Fun fact: "cyberpunks" are opportunistic computer hackers trying to challenge and overthrow an oppressive force. The name was coined by writer Bruce Bethke in 1980, and the name became so popular that people used it to refer to the genre itself, even if there aren't hackers in the story.

Examples of famous cyberpunk are *Neuromancer* by William Gibson, *Snow Crash* by Neal Stephenson, and *Do Androids Dream of Electric Sheep?* by Philip K. Dick.

See *Science Fiction*.

See also *Appendix C: Fiction Genres*.

Cryptocurrency

1. Decentralized digital currency not regulated by any bank

Cryptocurrency is a buzz word that will be an important part of our society as the technology evolves.

The digital currency has many allures: first, convenience; second, encrypted transactions, ensuring anonymity; and third, the ability to accept micropayments, such as paying for just one chapter of a book rather than the entire book—retailers can't offer this flexibility.

Combine these benefits with the power of blockchain and you have a transformative force that could completely change the way some industries do business, particularly banks, attorneys, real estate agents, and even authors and publishers. But you also have a force that can create legislative and financial headaches, as well as security concerns.

See *Blockchain* and *Digital Wallet.*

Customer Acquisition Cost (CAC)

1. The cost to acquire a new customer

Businesses try to keep their customer acquisition cost as low as possible in order to avoid cash flow problems.

D

Dedication

1. Front matter element where the author dedicates the book in someone's honor

See *Front Matter*.

See also *Appendix A: Front and Back Matter*.

Defamation

1. Act of damaging someone's reputation

Slander is spoken defamation, and libel is written defamation.

Authors have to be especially careful with defamation. For example, if you think another author is a terrible writer and you write a post on your blog about how terrible they are, and it damages their reputation, you could have a defamation lawsuit against you if the other author can prove that you made them lose sales. If you do podcast interviews or YouTube videos, be very careful about what you say about other authors. It could come back to haunt you.

Michael's opinion only: if you don't have anything nice to say, don't say anything at all.

Denouement

1. The final part of a story where loose ends are resolved; the resolution

From the French, pronounced "DAY-noo-mon".

See *Freytag's Pyramid*.

Developmental Editing

1. Type of editing in which an editor evaluates a story and makes high-level suggestions about the story structure and characters

Also known as a content edit, manuscript appraisal, structural edit, substantive edit, or book doctoring.

Generally, developmental editing is the most expensive editing you can buy. The editor is primarily concerned with whether the story elements work. They may recommend that you add, delete, or rewrite entire passages, remove or add certain character types, or even add entire plot lines.

See *Editing, Editor, Copyediting*, and *Proofreading*.

Delivery Cost

1. On Amazon, the cost to deliver an ebook file to a reader's reading device, subtracted from an author's royalty

Dictation

1. The act of writing a book through speaking the narrative into physical or digital software, which translates voice into text

Dictation has two forms. Some authors use digital recorders and dictate their stories while on walks; others use software such as Dragon by Nuance to speak directly into a writing program; others may simply use the built-in voice-to-text programs on their smartphones.

See *Transcription*.

Digital Rights Management (DRM)

1. A system of encryption that prevents unauthorized users from sharing copyrighted material

When a book is DRM-protected, the contents are encrypted so that only the person who bought the book can read it. DRM work cannot be copied or shared.

See *Copyright.*

Digital Wallet

1. App that stores credit card information or cryptocurrencies in order to make digital purchases

See *Cryptocurrency.*

Direct Sales

1. The act of selling books directly on a website, or in person

Indirect sales are sales that happen on a book retailer where the retailer takes a percentage of each sale, usually 30% to 40% for ebooks and paperbacks. In a direct sales payment model, the author uses a payment transaction service that takes a very small percentage of each transaction, usually less than 10%. The royalties are higher, and the author can sell unique and inventive products that they would not be able to sell through a book retailer, such as merchandise.

Disintermediation

1. The removal of intermediaries from a supply chain
   (known as "cutting out the middle man")

Disintermediation is most commonly used to describe the disruption of technology. For example, people historically used to go to a travel agent to book a vacation. But with the rise of websites and smartphone apps that allow people to book vacations without leaving their living room, travel agents have been disintermediated from the supply chain.

Technologies such as blockchain and artificial intelligence have the capability to disintermediate many jobs and transform entire industries.

See *Artficial Intelligence, Blockchain*, and *Smart Contract*.

Distributor

1. A company that distributes books from the
   publisher or author to book retailers

A distributor can distribute ebooks, paperbacks, or audiobooks, though they usually specialize in one format. For print books, a "full-service" distributor offers a range of services, such as sales, inventory management assistance, operating warehouses, and goods delivery.

At the time of this writing, Draft2Digital, PublishDrive,

and Streetlib are the most popular ebook distributors for indie writers, and Findaway Voices is the most popular distributor for audiobooks.

See *Book Retailer*, *Ebook Aggregator*, and *Independent Bookstore*.

Do Not Compete Clause

1. Clause in a publishing contract that bars an author from publishing any additional work that might compete with the book that the publisher is creating

The purpose of a do not compete clause is to protect the publisher's work. For example, if an author self-published a book in the same genre around the same time as the publisher's, then readers might buy the self-published book and not the traditionally-published one, thus hurting the publisher's sales.

Do not compete clauses can be quite draconian. The only way around them in most cases is to publish under a different pen name, usually in a different genre. Otherwise, the publisher could legally enforce the clause.

It goes without saying that these types of clauses can severely cripple a writer's career because they restrict what they can publish. It's best to avoid them whenever possible.

See *Appendix D: Copyright*.

Drop Caps

1. Large capital letter at the beginning of a chapter or
   section that occupies two lines

See *Small Caps*.

Dust Jacket

1. On a hardcover book, the detachable outer cover

Also known as a book jacket or dust cover. The opposite of a
dust jacket is a casewrap hardcover.

See *Casewrap*.

E

Ebook

1. A digital version of a book that is consumed in a browser, e-reader, or mobile device such as a smartphone or tablet

An ebook is a glorified HTML file. In fact, each chapter in an ebook is a sequence of HTML code, with a wrapper that tells a device how to display it.

See *Electronic Publication Format, e-reader, Mobipocket File, Portable Digital Format.*

Ebook Aggregator

1. Digital distributor who distributes copies of an author's book to many different retailers in exchange for a commission

Also known as ebook distributors.

Ebook aggregators help authors in two major ways. First, they create convenience because they distribute to many different retailers, so an author only has to publish the book on the ebook aggregator; the aggregator will send the book to places like Amazon, Kobo, Barnes & Noble, etc.

Second, ebook aggregators can distribute to smaller, regional retailers that authors don't have access to, particularly in international markets.

Ebook aggregators differ from print distributors in that they deal solely with ebooks. They don't distribute print books, and it's doubtful that they ever will since it's a completely different business model and print distributors serve publishers, not authors. This is why I've been careful to call them aggregators. But know that some people may refer to them as ebook distributors as well.

See *Distributor*.

Editing

1. The act of revising a written work's story, structure, spelling, and grammar until it meets the author's satisfaction.

See *Copyediting*, *Developmental Editing*, *Editor*, and *Proofreading*.

Editor

1. One who edits a manuscript for grammar, clarity, and continuity, usually paid by a publishing house or by an author directly

Editors come in different varieties and offer different services depending on their interests. Developmental editors work with an author to make the story elements crisper, and the work involves rearranging, rewriting, and deleting entire passages. Developmental editing is the most cost and time-intensive type of editing. Copyeditors work at the sentence level, fixing spelling, grammar, word choice, and clarity. And lastly, proofreaders check a manuscript for any remaining spelling and grammar errors that the other editors didn't catch or that were accidentally introduced by the author during the editing process.

It is not uncommon for an editor to offer one or all three of these services at different pricing levels.

Some editors specialize in certain genres while others have a generalist skillset.

Editing is a valuable skillset and many reputable editors belong to professional associations (such as the Society for Editors and Proofreaders) that provide best practices and resources for them to do their jobs more effectively and add value to their clients.

See *Copyediting*, *Developmental Editing*, *Editing*, and *Proofreading*.

Electronic Publication Format (ePUB)

1. Standardized ebook format, and the most widely used outside of Amazon

Authors can use a number of free and paid software programs to create ePUB files. A free example is Calibre, and a paid example is Scrivener.

. . .

See *Mobipocket File* and *Portable Digital Format.*

Ellipsis

1. Punctuation that signifies a trailing off or omission of words

An ellipsis is an effective punctuation tool, especially with dialogue.

For example, take the example "If you don't pay me by five o'clock, you'll be sorry..."

I've veiled a threat in the ellipsis.

You could also use an ellipsis as an omission, like if someone is talking a lot and the POV character tunes them out and starts to daydream.

There are other creative uses for an ellipsis. It's a very useful punctuation tool, but it's best used sparingly as it is often misused and misunderstood.

Embed

1. The act of placing media from one site (usually social media) directly onto another site

Embedding is a great and easy way to share social media content. The most common use of embedding occurs with video. Authors can embed video into blog articles, for example.

Disclaimer: Always remember that just because you can embed something doesn't mean you should. Beware of copyright infringement.

See *Infringement.*

Em Dash

1. Punctuation used in writing to signify a pause

Em dashes are common in fiction and nonfiction—they're great segues into explaining things, much like a colon. It is the longest dash.

See *En Dash.*

Endnotes

1. Back matter element in which an author cites references (may also appear in the book's body as footnotes)

Endnotes and footnotes are most common in nonfiction. Generally, a book will have footnotes that appear on the page where they are cited, or endnotes, where all the references are listed in a single section.

. . .

See *Back Matter* and *Bibliography*.

See also *Appendix A: Front and Back Matter.*

En dash

1. Punctuation tool used in writing numbers and
   formulations

Whereas the em dash is used as a punctuation tool, the en dash
is used to show relationships between numerical data, like
dates. For example, when you are writing a date range, an en
dash is most appropriate. June 1, 2015–June 5, 2016.

The en dash is shorter than an em dash but longer than a
hyphen. Technically speaking, an en dash is the width of the
letter "n" and an em dash is the width of an "m", but that's
oversimplifying it.

For an easy way to remember the difference between an em
dash and an en dash, remember that the "n" in en dash means
numbers.

See *Em Dash.*

Epigraph

1. Front matter element that uses a quote or song lyric
   to set the mood of the book

Epigraphs are commonly confused with epigrams, which are short and pithy sayings.

See *Front Matter.*

See also *Appendix A: Front and Back Matter.*

Epilogue

1. In a novel, back matter element with the conclusion of a story that takes place after the main plot has ended

See *Back Matter* and *Conclusion.*

See also *Appendix A: Front and Back Matter.*

E-reader

1. A device that displays ebooks; usually a dedicated device but also includes smartphones and tablets

The Kindle was the first and (still) most prominent e-reader device. It used e-ink technology to create a paper-like experience. Over the years, dedicated e-readers have fallen somewhat out of favor as more people prefer to read on their smart-phones and tablets.

Also stylized as e-reader.

See *Ebook* and *Kindle*.

Erotica

1. Genre in which sex is the focus of the plot and whose goal is to arouse sexual desire

See *Appendix C: Fiction Genres.*

Exposition

1. Descriptive text that explains something
2. In Freytag's pyramid, the beginning of the story structure where the hero, setting, and stakes are introduced

For definition #1, in a novel, any time the narrator is describing something or explaining how they feel or think, that's exposition.

In a nonfiction book, pretty much everything an author writes is exposition.

For definition #2: Writers rarely use exposition in the context of Freytag's Pyramid. Unless specifically defined, always assume definition #1.

See *Freytag's Pyramid*.

F

Fair Use

1. In copyright law, the doctrine that brief excerpts of a work can be used for the purposes of review, discussion, or criticism without asking the copyright holder for permission

Fair use is too complex to discuss in this book. See the Appendix for a great book that discusses it and all things copyright.

See *Copyright* and *Creative Commons*.

Fantasy

1. Fiction genre that takes place in (usually) an imaginative world, with magic, magical settings, and magical creatures

To use the most common examples of fantasy, The Lord of the Rings and Harry Potter are examples of fantasy. They feature magic, magical creatures, and a story where the good guys win. Fantasy is a wide-ranging genre with many, many subgenres and flavors.

See *Appendix C: Fiction Genres*.

Final Battle

1. Climax of a story where the hero faces off against
   the villain

See *Freytag's Pyramid* and *Plot*.

First Rights

1. The exclusive right to publish a work for the
   first time

Literary magazines commonly purchase first rights for short
stories so that they are the first ones to print the work. Traditional publishers also buy first rights to the novels they publish
(among many other rights).

See *Foreign Rights*, *Secondary Rights*, *Subsidiary Rights*, and *World English Rights*.

Fleisch-Kincaid Score

1. A score that gauges the readability of a text

The Fleisch-Kincaid score is commonly used on websites to show how readable the copy is. It may also have uses in nonfiction writing.

Fiction writers, however, should stay well away from it.

Folio

1. The page number in a printed book

Font

1. A set of a typeface and size used in a manuscript or a book cover (i.e. Times New Roman or Garamond)

It is a little known fact that fonts are copyrighted. Some fonts are open-source; for others, you must get a license to use it from the creator of the font. Authors and cover designers can get into trouble by using unlicensed fonts on their covers, so it is always wise to ask your designer what fonts they use in your design and whether they hold the necessary license.

Michael's opinion only: when in doubt, pay for a copy of the license yourself.

See *Monospaced Font, Sans Serif Font, Serif Font,* and *Typography*.

Foreign Rights

1. Translation rights licensed by an author to a
    publisher

See *First Rights*, *Secondary Rights*, *Subsidiary Rights*, and *World
English Rights*.

Foreword

1. Front matter element in which the author or
    someone prominent comments on the book and its
    significance

In fiction, forewords are most commonly written by someone
other than the author, such as a bestseller in the genre. It is rare
to see this except in the case of a book that is selling very well
or has been for decades.

In nonfiction, forewords can be written by someone else of
prominence or by the author, especially if the book is a new
edition. The climate in which the author wrote the book may
have changed since the last edition, so it is often customary for
them to comment on that in order to set the tone for the book
as well as outline any sections that have been changed or
updated.

See *Author's Note*, *Front Matter*, *Introduction*, and *Preface*.

See *Appendix A: Front and Back Matter*.

Fragment

1. An incomplete sentence

Frame

1. Storytelling technique where a story is told within a story

Freelancing

1. Employment style in which one works for multiple clients on a per-job basis instead of receiving a salary from just one company

Let's say that you are a journalist who writes blog articles.

In a salaried employment structure, you receive a salary in exchange for working exclusively for one company. You also receive benefits such as health insurance. So if you work for the local newspaper and they pay you to write for them and only them, you are probably an employee.

In a freelancing employment structure, one is not tied to any single employer. So you could write articles for the local newspaper on a per-article basis and also for a dozen or so online blogs. They pay you per word, you have more flexibility to control your schedule, but you do not receive health insurance.

In self-publishing, editors and cover designers are classic examples of people who generally work on a freelance basis.

. . .

See *Collaborative Consumption* and *Work for Hire*.

Freewriting

1. Creativity exercise where the author free associates and writes whatever is on their mind

Freewriting can be an effective technique to combat writer's block and boost your creativity.

See *Character Sketch*.

See also *Appendix B: Resources for More Learning*.

Freytag's Pyramid

1. Universal plot structure that consists of exposition, initial incident, rising action, climax, falling action, resolution, and denouement

See *Anti-climactic*, *Climax*, and *Denouement*.

Frontispiece

1. Front matter element that contains an illustration that faces the title page

See *Front Matter.*

See also *Appendix A: Front and Back Matter.*

Frontlist

1. An author's most recently released work

See *Backlist.*

Front Matter

1. Elements of a book that appear immediately before the body

The title page, copyright page, foreword, frontispiece, and dedication are examples of front matter.

Also known as prelims.

See *Back Matter.*

See also *Appendix A: Front and Back Matter.*

G

General Data Protection Regulation (GDPR)

1. Strict set of European Union regulations that govern privacy how businesses use and store personal information

The GDPR is a morass of regulation, and there's nothing else quite like it. If you don't live in the EU, it still applies to you if you process transactions from customers who do live in the EU, or if you have EU customers on your email list, for example. A detailed discussion of GDPR is outside the scope of this book, as the regulation will continue to evolve over time.

Get Things Done Method (GTD)

1. Management methodology created by David Allen to help boost productivity while minimizing stress

See *Pomodoro Method*.

Ghostwriting

1. The act of writing a novel for someone else, usually without attribution

Individuals who want to build a brand but don't necessarily have the time or skill to write hire ghostwriters. So do celebrities.

Ghostwriters must usually sign a non-disclosure agreement (NDA), since if it were known that the titled author on the book didn't in fact write it, reputational damage could occur. The work ghostwriters create is usually work for hire as well, with the titled author owning the copyright, though this can sometimes be negotiated.

See *Non-Disclosure Agreement* and *Work for Hire*.

Glossary

1. Back matter element with terms and definitions used in the book

In nonfiction, glossaries help readers keep terms straight. In fiction, they're quite rare, but may be used in genres such as epic fantasy to help readers keep terms or fictional language words straight.

See *Appendix*, *Back Matter*, and *Index*.
    See also *Appendix A: Front and Back Matter*.

Go Direct

1. To publish an ebook directly to a book retailer without using a distributor or aggregator

See *Ebook Aggregator* and *Go Wide*.

Going Wide

1. In self-publishing, the act of publishing a book on as many retailers as possible instead of being exclusive to Amazon

See *Ebook Aggregator, Go Direct*, and *Kindle Direct Publishing Select.*

Graphic Interchange Format File (GIF)

1. Image format that supports static and animated images

GIF is pronounced "jiff".

GIFs can be animated, and for this reason, they lend themselves well to social media and text messages. For images that will be used on websites or for other high-resolution purposes, see *Joint Photographic Experts Group Graphic File (JPEG)* and *Portable Network Graphic File (PNG)*.

Grant of License

1. In a publishing contract, the clause that outlines

what rights the author is signing over to the
publisher

Also known as a Grant of Rights.

See *Life-of-Copyright Contract*, *Moral Rights*, *Subsidiary Rights*, and
World English Rights.

See also *Appendix D: Copyright*.

Gutter

1. In a printed book, the margin on the inside of
each page

See *Margin*.

Half Title

1. Front matter element containing the title of the book, most often used when the book's front matter is long

Also known as a Second Half Title since it appears in addition to the title page.

See *Front Matter* and *Second Half Title*.

See also *Appendix A: Front and Back Matter*.

Happily Ever After (HEA)

1. In romance novels, an ending where all loose ends are wrapped up neatly, the heroine and the hero are in love and together, and that generally makes readers feel good

Happily Ever After endings are required in romance. Readers demand them. If a story does not have a HEA, it is not a romance.

See *Romance*.

Heinlein's Rules

1. Series of rules invented by Robert A. Heinlein that illustrate how to become a successful writer

Heinlein's Rules are as follows (paraphrased):
1. You must write.
2. You must finish what you write.
3. You must not rewrite, unless an editor demands it.
4. You must put your work on the market
5. You must keep it on the market until it sells

These five simple rules are simple, but they certainly aren't easy.

See *Appendix B: Resources for More Learning.*

Hero's Journey

1. Plot structure popularized by Joseph Campbell's *Hero With a Thousand Faces*

The Hero's Journey is one of the most popular and widely recognized plotting methods.

See *Appendix B: Resources for More Learning.*

Historical Fiction

1. Genre that takes place in historical times

Historical fiction is a popular genre that encompasses virtually every fiction subgenre and every historical time. The hallmark of the genre is that it weaves fiction with actual historical events. Readers are very particular about the accuracy of the historical details.

See *Appendix C: Fiction Genres.*

Hook

1. In fiction, an element of the plot that gets the reader's attention
2. In copywriting, a phrase or word that gets the reader's attention

See *Marketing.*

Horror

1. Fiction genre written with the intent to evoke feelings of horror

Classic examples of horror include *Dracula* by Bram Stoker, *The Tell-Tale Heart* by Edgar Allen Poet, and *It* by Stephen King, Horror can encompass all fiction subgenres and is often blended with other elements such as post-apocalyptic settings.

See *Appendix C: Fiction Genres.*

House Ad

1. An ad that you run on your own website to promote one of your books or services

Hybrid Author

1. An author who has books that are traditionally-published and self-published

Commonly confused with hybrid publisher.

See *Hybrid Publisher.*

Hybrid Publisher

1. A publisher who provides a mix of traditional and self-publishing services, usually in the same contract

Commonly confused with Hybrid Author.

A hybrid publisher may help an author self-publish their book, for example, but may take a percentage of royalties in exchange for the assistance.

This is a relatively new field that is fraught with contractual dangers, so always use a watchdog service like The Alliance of Independent Authors when deciding on whether a hybrid publishing service is legitimate or not.

See *Assisted Self-Publisher, Hybrid Author,* and *Vanity Publisher.*

I

Impressions

1. The number of times an ad is served (but not necessarily seen)

See *Conversion* and *Pay-Per-Click Advertising.*

Imprint

1. Division of a publisher that prints a certain type of books, usually in a particular genre

For example, Penguin Books has many imprints. Penguin Classics publishes literary classics and books from the public domain, and DAW publishes science fiction and fantasy. Each imprint has different branding.

Sometimes publishers create imprints to differentiate their product offerings, or they may purchase other publishers and use them as imprints.

See *"Big Five" Publishers* and *Traditional Publisher.*

Income Stream

1. Money flowing into a business

Indie authors have many income streams by virtue of their business model. Each book is an income stream, and each format of the book (ebook, paperback, audio, translation, etc.) is also an income stream. Every retailer you publish at is an income stream, and so are alternative sources of income like affiliate income, direct sales at conventions, and even income through a site like Patreon.

Also known as revenue stream.

See *Active Income*, *Cash Flow*, *Merchandising*, and *Passive Income*.

Independent Bookstore

1. An independently-owned bookstore that is self-reliant in bringing customers into the store

Your local bookstore is an independent bookstore. Your local Barnes & Noble/Chapters/Waterstones/etc. is not. They are franchised and can draw upon the power of their brand and ability to open very large locations at malls and shopping centers to bring in foot traffic. A local independent bookstore doesn't have that kind of capital or power, but it does have knowledgeable booksellers who can provide better service and choices for readers.

See *Book Retailer* and *Distributor*.

Independent (Indie) Publisher

1. A trade publishing house not affiliated with a large corporate conglomerate
2. An author who publishes their work independent of a publishing company; a self-published author or indie author

Historically, the term "indie publisher" referred to publishing houses, but with the rise of self-publishing, indie authors have adopted the term to describe themselves.

See *Authorpreneur, Self-Publishing,* and *Trade Publishing.*

Index

1. Back matter element that references the page number of all special terms that appear in the book

An index differs from a glossary in that it is strictly a reference of where the terms appear, whereas a glossary defines the terms.

See *Front Matter* and *Glossary.*

See also *Appendix A: Front and Back Matter.*

Influencer

1. An individual with a large following on a blog, podcast, or social media site, usually with the ability to influence their followers to buy or not buy a product, and to act or not act upon something, such as a petition

See *Content Marketing*, *Microinfluencer*, and *Platform*.

Infringement

1. A violation of the rights of another, such as a copyright or trademark

Authors should be careful not to use any images, photos, song lyrics, artwork, or any other copyrightable material without the copyright owner's permission. As a second precaution, they should make sure that if permission is granted and that the person granting permission actually has the authority to do so. For example, in the case of photos, there have been many cases where people have used images on their websites or blogs that they thought had permission for, but the grantor was in fact infringing on the copyright of another by passing the images off as their own.

Authors should also be careful to avoid using trademarks in their work, such as on their book cover, in their book titles or keywords, in the text of the book itself, and any other place that might lead readers to mistakenly believe that the author is associated with the mark.

See *Copyright, Piracy, Trademark, Trade Dress*, and *Intellectual Property*.

Intellectual Property

1. Property of an intangible nature, usually creative such as a written work, composition, artwork, a slogan or an invention

See *Copyright, Trademark*, and *Trade Dress*.

Interior

1. The content on the inside of an ebook or paperback (as opposed to the book cover, which is the exterior)

Also known as a book block.

Sometimes, in a copyright page, an author may choose to specify the copyright of the work, attributing the cover copyright to the cover designer and the interior copyright (the book itself) to the author.

See *Copyright Page*.

International Standard Book Number (ISBN)

1. A unique numeric identifier attached to a book that makes it possible to be found in databases

An ISBN has a number of uses. For starters, you need one to have your book distributed into physical bookstores.

However, for ebooks, they are optional as all retailers will let you publish without one.

If you do use an ISBN, you are required to use a different ISBN for each edition of the book, meaning if your book is available in paperback and audio, you would need to use a separate ISBN for each.

ISBNs can have 10 or 13 digits. Much like a VIN on a car, each digit has a meaning, but that's outside the scope of this book.

ISBNs are country-specific and can only be issued by an appointed agency in each country.

Nielsen provides reports on the publishing industry each year, and they base their reports on books that have ISBNs, including ebooks. As a result, since many indie authors do not use ISBNs for their ebooks, the indie world is somewhat of a "shadow industry" that isn't tracked on any official reports.

Unlike the Amazon Standard Identification Number (ASIN), an ISBN can be used on any retailer. The only caveat is that some retailers such as Amazon and Draft2Digital issue free ISBNs if the author doesn't have their own, which makes it easy to publish on those retailers—but the catch is that the retailer will be listed as the publisher of record for the ISBN, not the author. As such, for competition reasons, other retailers won't accept an ISBN with another retailer's name on it.

. . .

See *Amazon Standard Identification Number*.

Introduction

1. In nonfiction, a front matter element where the
   author explains the reason for writing the work

An introduction differs from a foreword in that a foreword is usually written by someone other than the author.

In case of confusion, an introduction is similar to a preface. It probably doesn't make sense to include both in a book, so pick the name that works best and use that.

See *Author's Note*, *Front Matter*, and *Preface*.

See also *Appendix A: Front and Back Matter*.

In Media Res

1. Latin for "in the midst of things"; the act of starting
   a novel in the middle of an action scene

See *Cold Open*.

J

Joint Photographic Experts Group File (JPEG)

1. File format commonly used for digital photos

A technical explanation of JPEG files is beyond the scope of this book, but it tends to be the ideal format for photos and web graphics.

See *Graphic Interface Exchange Format (GIF)* and *Portable Network Graphic File (PNG)*.

Justification

1. The arrangement of text on the page, generally in relation to the right margin

Justification is commonly confused with alignment. Justification generally refers to the right margin and how it looks. In a paperback book, it is highly desirable because every line ends at the same spot on the right margin, and therefore looks cleaner. The opposite of this is "ragged right," where the ends of each line stop at different points, depending on how many characters are in the line.

See *Alignment* and *Margin*.

K

Kindle

1. Amazon's physical e-reader or tablet that can be used to read ebooks
2. App by Amazon that can be installed on computers, phones, and tablets to read ebooks

See *Ebook* and *E-reader*.

Kindle Unlimited (KU)

1. Amazon's monthly subscription program where readers pay one monthly fee in exchange for unlimited access to all books enrolled in the Kindle Unlimited program; authors are paid for every page read

See *Kindle Direct Publishing (KDP) Select*.

Kindle Direct Publishing (KDP) Select

1. Amazon's exclusive publishing program that offers algorithmic and marketing benefits (including Kindle Unlimited) for a book in exchange for exclusivity to the Amazon ecosystem

See *Going Wide* and *Kindle Unlimited*.

L

Launch

1. The process of making a book public for the first time

Launches are important events in the life of every book. Authors usually plan them weeks if not months in advance so that they can book promotions at promo sites, arrange newsletter swaps, send advance reader copies to early readers and book bloggers, and other promotional activities.

A "hard launch" is when the author communicates the book's release immediately when it becomes available. A "soft launch" is when the author publishes the book, but waits a period of time to start talking about it while they wait for early reviews and sales. The goal of a soft launch is to have some social proof before the major promotions begin.

See *Social Proof* and *Promotion.*

Law of Diminishing Returns

1. In any given business activity, when the amount of return is more than the money invested, but with repetition becomes less profitable

A classic example of diminishing returns with indie authors is with book promotion sites. You can only promote your book to the same group of people before they tire of it. The first time you promote a book to a list of readers, you may see a nice sales bump. But the next time you promote that book, you'll usually see fewer sales.

Lead Magnet

1. In marketing, a free item that a business gives away in order to entice customers to sign up for an email list, such as a white paper, free book, or webinar

In the writing community, lead magnets are referred to as "reader magnets", popularized by Nick Stephenson's book *Reader Magnets.*

For authors, a reader magnet is usually a free book or a short story.

See *Loss Leader*, *Mailing List*, and *Sales Funnel*.

Lester Dent Plot Formula

1. Plot structure popularized by pulp writer Lester Dent, useful for mystery short stories

See *Appendix B: Resources for More Learning.*

License

1. The right to use a copyrighted work for a certain purpose; granted by the copyright holder

In legal terms, licensing is also known as encumbering.

See *Grant of License, Foreign Rights, Subsidiary Rights,* and *World English Rights.*

Life-of-Copyright Contract

1. A contract that is valid for the entire life of the copyright of the work

Life-of-copyright contracts can be devastating for a writer. It is best to avoid them at all costs.

List Price

1. The recommended retail price (RRP) of a book, set by the author or publisher

Literary Agent

1. One who represents authors and sells prospective manuscripts to book publishers

In the world of self-publishing, literary agents are not necessary to have a successful career since authors can bypass agents and publishers altogether and market their work directly to readers.

See *Agency Clause* and *Boutique Agency*.

LitRPG

1. Short for "literary roleplaying game," a genre that usually takes place inside a video game and relies heavily on roleplaying game characteristics

See *Appendix C: Fiction Genres*.

Loss Leader

1. A product sold at a loss to attract customers

Grocery stores use loss leaders all the time, such as buy one get one free offers on certain foods to get shoppers in the store. Once shoppers are in the store, they'll usually spend more money, which will help the grocery store make up for the loss leader.

Authors do this primarily through steeply discounting an introductory book to a very low price or free.

· · ·

See *Lead Magnet* and *Permafree*.

M

Mailing List

1. An email list where subscribers sign up for updates from a business, usually in exchange for a free gift

Also known as a newsletter or fan club.

See *Autoresponder, Call to Action, Campaign, Click Rate, Conversion, Lead Magnet, Open Rate, Opt-In, Opt-Out,* and *Squeeze Page.*

Margin

1. In business, the difference between the cost to create a product and the selling price
2. In formatting, the edge of the printable section of a page

For definition #1, let's say A product costs $1.00. It is sold for $10.00, so it would have a 90% margin, which is exceedingly good.

Knowing margin is important when selling a paperback title because you have to factor in the selling price minus the cost to print the book, taxes, and shipping.

For business, see *Markup, Overhead, Return on Investment.*

. . .

For formatting, see *Alignment*, *Bleed*, *Gutter*, and *Justification*.

Marketing

1. The act of selling a product or service

Marketing differs from promotion in that it is primarily about connecting with a target audience, crafting a message to speak to that audience, and creating packaging that will appeal to them. Promotion is the act of promoting the book to that audience, such as through advertising.

See *Hook*, *Press Kit*, and *Promotion*.

Markdown

1. A formatting syntax designed for easy export to HTML

Many writing apps support Markdown.

See *Appendix B: Resources for More Learning*.

Markup

1. In business, the difference between the cost of a product and its selling price
2. In formatting, the process of editing a manuscript before publication

For definition #1, let's say that we have a product that costs $3.00 to make and sells for $5.00. For every product you sell, you make a profit of $2.00, which is a 67% markup, which you can calculate by dividing $5.00 by $3.00.

For business, see *Margin*.

Mass Market Paperback

1. Books printed for large audiences, usually with large print runs

Mass market paperbacks are smaller than trade paperbacks, usually 4 inches by 7 inches. Surging in popularity after World War II, they were designed to fit into a purse or pocket.

Without a publisher, it is nearly impossible for an indie author to put their books into mass market format because the format requires very large print runs.

See *Print On-Demand* and *Trade Paperback*.

Master of Fine Arts (MFA)

1. Master's degree in a creative field that qualifies the holder to teach in that field

Typically, authors who write literary fiction may hold MFAs. It qualifies you to teach writing at a university, nothing more, nothing less. It is not needed for non-literary fiction writing, though some universities offer commercial fiction programs.

Michael La Ronn's opinion only: you don't need it. Invest that money instead into your career.

Merchandising

1. In book sales, the act of hand-selecting books to be featured prominently in a bookstore or an online retailer
2. In business, the act of creating affiliated products such as t-shirts, cups, mugs, or other products associated with a business's brand beyond their flagship products or content

For definition #1, merchandising is how bookstores make their money. By featuring some books at the front of the store, they could sell more of them. The same goes at online retailers— any time you see big banners advertising new series or "summer reads," that's merchandising.

For definition #2, merchandising and creating different

types of products is a great way to create another income stream.

See *Income Stream*.

Metadata

1. A set of data that describes other data

When you are uploading your book to sell through a retailer, you have to enter certain items: title, author name, book description, keywords, etc. Each of those elements is metadata. It describes your book so that 1) the retailer can place it in the appropriate place on a physical or digital shelf, and 2) so readers can find your book, know who wrote it, and what it is about. Don't ignore or underestimate the power of metadata, especially your book description, keywords, and categories. They can help your book be discovered.

See *Book Industry Standards and Communication and Category*.

Microinfluencer

1. An individual with a small following on a blog, podcast, or social media site, usually with the ability to influence their followers to buy or not buy a product, and to act or not act upon something, such as a petition; usually 1,000 people or less

What constitutes the "size" of a microinfluencer is still up for debate, but someone with one million fans is definitely NOT a microinfluencer.

On their own, a microinfluencer doesn't have much influence. But as a block, they may be able to reach more people collectively than one big influencer, which is why brands like to work with them.

See *Content Marketing*, *Influencer*, and *Platform*.

Middle Grade

1. Novels written for children ages 8-12

See *Young Adult*.

Midlist

1. A traditionally-published segment of books that are not bestsellers but perform well enough to be financially viable for the publisher

See *Midlist Author*.

Midlist Author

1. A traditionally-published author who is not a bestseller but who makes enough money for his/her publisher

See *Midlist.*

Military Science Fiction

1. Science fiction told from the perspective of a hero who serves or has served in the armed forces

Military science fiction spans all genres, but is particularly prominent in the space genre and commonly confused with space opera.

See *Appendix C: Fiction Genres.*

Mindmap

1. A visual representation of an idea, usually through a web of associated thoughts and topics

Minimum Viable Product (MVP)

1. In business, a product that is brought to market

without having been fully optimized but that exists to prove whether people will buy it

2. In publishing, the act of writing the first few chapters of a book and getting feedback from trusted readers to determine if the book is worth continuing; if readers provide negative feedback, the book is either fixed until it is suitable for the market, or discontinued

In some cases, definition #1 is used to publish an unedited book on the market and use reader reviews for feedback. Michael La Ronn's opinion only: that's a bad idea. This works in business because a physical product still has a level of usefulness that the consumers find helpful, like a computer program or an electronic appliance, for example. That's not the case with a book. Many readers find it hard to enjoy a story if it's full of typos and consistency errors.

See *Alpha Reader*.

Mobipocket File (MOBI)

1. Standardized ebook format

Amazon's proprietary Kindle format is based on the **MOBI** architecture. The difference between a **MOBI** and an ePub is so slight that you can easily convert between the two formats without hardly any loss in quality. There are definite technical differences, but they are not likely to matter to an indie author.

As of 2021, MOBI files are no longer required to upload a book to Amazon, but the format is still needed to read books on legacy Kindle devices.

See *Ebook*, *Electronic Publication Format,* and *Portable Digital Format.*

Model Release

1. In photography, a waiver of liability granted by a model in a photo shoot so that the photographer has the right to use their photo for commercial purposes

Model releases are important for authors in a couple of areas. First, it's always best practice for a cover designer to use stock photo images for which a model release exists. Some retailers even keep releases for photographers.

In the event that the model is a minor and the photographer didn't realize it, or the model claims that they did not authorize the sale of a stock photo and selling it is an invasion of their privacy, this protects the author, the cover designer, and the retailer where the designer purchases the image.

Second, a model release is important when an author is buying stock photo images to use on their blogs, ads, etc. Knowing that a model in a given stock photo has released their rights is an added layer of assurance that the retailer has the right to license the image, has secured the appropriate permissions, and that there is no risk of copyright infringement.

While model releases are not always possible to get, they are important.

See *Model Release*, *Moral Rights*, *Royalty-Free*, and *Stock Content*.

Monospaced Font

1. A font in which each character takes up the exact same amount of horizontal space on a page (as opposed to a proportionally spaced font)

Courier is a classic monospaced font. Editors of literary magazines often require these types of fonts in their submission process because it is easier to spot typos with a monospaced font, and writing is more legible. Computer programmers code with monospaced fonts for this reason too.

See *Font*, *Sans Serif Font* and *Serif Font*.

Moral Rights

1. The collective rights of an author separate from copyright that give them unique rights, such as the right to be attributed on a work, the right to have a work published anonymously, and the right of integrity, which is the ability to object to any alteration of the work that would damage the author's reputation

Moral rights are separate from copyright and economic rights to a work. Unlike copyright, which is transferred via contract, moral rights cannot be separated (or "alienated") from the author.

In countries that observe moral rights (the UK and continental Europe, for example), the work cannot be alienated from the author. When the author signs a publishing contract, they still retain their moral rights. If an author objects to how the publisher uses the work, they have a legal path to take back the rights to the work under the legal theory that the publisher may be destroying the work's integrity, and therefore damaging the artistic reputation of the author.

In countries that do not observe moral rights (like the United States), the author and the rights *can* be alienated, meaning that someone who obtains the rights can do whatever they want with the work without fear of action from the author. In this case, if an author does not like how a publisher uses the work, they're out of luck unless they skillfully negotiated their contract. To change gears slightly, a great example of how this can happen is as follows: let's say the author doesn't negotiate in a movie deal that their name must be included in a movie's trailers, opening and ending credits, which is a costly mistake for the author because they miss out on a prime marketing opportunity. The author can only sue if attribution was a contractual condition and the movie studio breached the contract. If the author were a citizen of a country that observes moral rights, attribution would be required as a matter of law. If the movie studio did not attribute the author in the film, the author could take legal action.

Moral rights are quite complicated and I can't do them justice here. Their power depends on what country you live in. Europe has historically championed moral rights while the

United States has largely ignored them, although that may be changing in the coming decades.

See *Intellectual Property*.

Mystery

1. Genre in which a protagonist solves a murder

See *Cozy Mystery* and *Appendix C: Fiction Genres.*

N

National Novel Writing Month (NaNoWriMo)

1. Annual initiative from November 1 through November 30 that challenges writers to write a 50,000-word novel in 30 days

Native Content

1. Content designed specifically for a particular social media site

With a native content approach, you create Instagram content just for Instagram, Facebook content just for Facebook, etc., following each website's general rules and media specifications. This helps your content get a better reach, and is preferable to using a scheduling app that pushes your content out to many different social media networks with little regard to how the content will appear on those networks. Whenever possible, creating native content is always better.

See *Content Marketing*.

Navigational Control for XML (NCX)

1. Ebook feature that allows readers to see the navigation of a book at any time, and jump freely between chapters

The NCX is a must-have feature in your ebook that readers demand. The NCX differs from the table of contents in that the table of contents is a page, whereas the NCX is a navigational feature.

See *Table of Contents*.

Narrator

1. The person narrating a book or a narrative within a book; may or may not be the viewpoint character
2. One who records an audiobook

See *Audiobook*.

New Adult (NA)

1. Genre that blends coming-of-age stories with romance, usually with protagonists age 18-30

New Adult is about the hero fighting the villain while also navigating coming into their own. Sexuality, college (or not), and learning to be an adult are major themes in new adult fiction. It encompasses all genres, particularly urban fantasy.

.   .   .

See *Urban Fantasy* and *Young Adult*.

Niche

1. A segment of the market whose audience has specialized interests and tastes

Niche is primarily a nonfiction term. For example, this very book appeals to the writing niche, for indie authors with 0-5 books who want to learn more about self-publishing.

You can't really achieve that level of specificity with fiction, but an example of a niche in fiction might be, for example, readers who like dark space opera along the lines of X author.

See *Target Audience*.

Noir

1. Crime genre characterized by cynicism, gritty settings and characters, and a stylized tone (i.e. Hardboiled detective)

See *Appendix C: Fiction Genres*.

Non-Disclosure Agreement (NDA)

1. Contract between two or more parties in which
   they agree not to disclose confidential information
   shared between them in order to accomplish a
   project or business venture

Legal settlements frequently include NDAs so that the parties
can't talk about the terms of the settlement. Usually, to do so
would expose things that one or more of the parties would
prefer not to have public, such as the amount of the settlement.

Ghostwriters also frequently have to sign non-disclosure
agreements so as not to expose the fact that the person they are
writing for didn't actually write the book they purported to.

See *Ghostwriting*.

Novel

1. A fictional story told in long-form

What constitutes a novel and how long is it? Those are fighting
words, and often debated. My opinion is that a novel can be
anywhere from 30,000 words and above, but a lot of people
have opinions about this.

I define a novella as anything over 10,000 words but under
30,000, and a short story as anything under 10,000. But that's
not a hard or fast rule.

Often, the structure technique matters too. Novels and novellas are typically broken into chapters.

The narrative techniques also differ. Short stories typically have one or two focuses. Novellas and novels tend to have a longer narrative that doesn't resolve after a few thousand words.

See *Chapter* and *Short Story*.

Offset Printing

1. The act of printing a book in bulk through a series of print runs, usually in large quantities and with greater flexibility on the outcome of the finished product

Unlike print on-demand, offset printing works by printing large batches of a book at a time, and it can be quite expensive, as an author has to invest this money upfront. However, the trade-off is that you have far more flexibility in how your book looks and the knowledgeable expertise of a printer who can help.

Offset printing is how traditional publishers print their books. The option is too cost-prohibitive for most indie authors, though some authors have seen success in doing limited-edition print runs of novels to sell to their true fans.

See *Print On-Demand* and *Print Run*.

Open Rate

1. An email marketing statistic that measures the percentage of people who open any given newsletter or autoresponder

See *Click Rate*, *Conversion*, and *Mailing List*.

Optical Character Recognition (OCR)

1. An ability of computer software to recognize printed characters on physical paper and translate it faithfully in a digital format

OCR is important in a number of scenarios. First, it is used in scanning print books to digital, and this was an essential element of the ebook revolution, as publishers needed to digitize their massive catalogues.

Second, say you take a lot of handwritten notes and need to get them into a digital format. It's too time-intensive to type your written words one-by-one. While not perfect, a computer can often do this faster.

See *Transcription*.

Option Clause (or Contract)

1. Contract clause (or contract) in which a grantor (such as a film studio) pays an author money in exchange for the exclusive right to develop certain content based on the work (such as a film) within a limited time period

The most common example of option contracts is in film. A film studio pays an author money to keep the film rights off the table to other film studios for a period of, say, five years. If the studio decides to develop a film during that period, additional talks and contracts commence. If the film decides not to develop a film during that period, they can either renew their option or let it expire. In the case of the latter, the author is then free to sell the film rights to another studio.

See *Appendix D: Copyright.*

Opt-In

1. The act of granting consent to a business to send communications, usually emails

Opt-ins are a must in today's digital economy where people are protective of their email inboxes. Businesses offer a number of incentives to customers in exchange for their email, such as coupons, free content, and free services. Email lists are valuable because the business can email its customers any time it has a new product or major announcement, thus improving sales.

A "single" opt-in is when a customer must enter their email address once in order to receive the incentive. This usually happens on the business's website, and once done, the customer is on the email list.

A "double" opt-in is when a customer must enter their email address and then click a link via email to verify that the business does in fact have their permission to email them. Double opt-ins are more work for the customer, but the business can be certain that their customer list has given them permission to communicate.

Failing to obtain customer's permission prior to emailing is illegal in some countries and can even lead to lawsuits. Legal consequences or not, it is generally frowned upon and unethical.

See *Mailing List* and *Opt-Out*.

Opt-Out

1. The act of unsubscribing from a business's email list

Also known as unsubscribe.

Customers may choose to be on a business's email list for any reason, and they may also choose to leave for any reason. Businesses usually offer a way for customers to "unsubscribe" and stop receiving emails. Many businesses track their unsubscribe rates as an indicator of whether their email content is relevant.

As with opt-ins, failing to offer an easy way to unsubscribe can also result in broken laws and lawsuits.

See *Mailing List* and *Opt-In*.

Organic Search

1. The act of users entering a search term in a search engine and happening upon content naturally

Also known as natural search. Organic search is important because it's free. You don't have to pay for it. If you have a tea review blog, customers are searching for "tea review blogs," and they happen to find your blog and consume your content and become a fan, your customer acquisition cost is zero. You didn't need to pay for an ad to drive traffic to your website.

For fiction writers, the only organic search they'll likely enjoy is when readers are searching for their name or one of their books.

For nonfiction writers, organic search should be a key pillar in the discoverability strategy. Nonfiction writers can create blog articles, podcasts, and videos that speak to topics that people their target market are actively searching for.

See *Search Engine Optimization.*

Outlining

1. In fiction, the process of working out the story, plot, and characters of a novel prior to writing
2. In nonfiction, the process of mapping out the major ideas and main points of a book prior to writing

In fiction, outlining is a useful skill as a writer, and writers fall into two camps: plotters and pantsers. Whether you outline or not, there is no right or wrong way to write a novel.

In nonfiction, outlining is perhaps more important to make sure that the book meets the needs of the writer's target audience.

. . .

See *Pantsing* and *Appendix B: Resources for More Learning* for useful resources on outlining.

Out-of-Print (OOP)

1. The unavailability of a book to be purchased

Overhead

1. All ongoing expenses a business must incur in order to offer its products or services

Taxes, insurance, rent, and utilities are common overhead expenses for a traditional business. Whether the business makes a profit or not, these expenses will continue forever.

For an author, overhead expenses will look a little different. Most indie authors work from their home and do not have insurance. Taxes vary from year to year and is not something we can plan for. We don't have true overhead expenses, per se, because nothing is required and almost nothing we do in this profession has an ongoing cost.

But for a professional indie author, overhead costs might include: website hosting, the cost to pay assistants for essential services such as bookkeeping, and any costs for professional organizations (if they use those organizations to form connections that lead to sales). If they're consistent, book covers and editing expenses could also be considered overhead. But again, what constitutes "overhead" for one author might be completely optional or unnecessary for another.

. . .

See *Margin.*

P

Pacing

1. The speed at which the events in a book progress

Pacing happens at the story, paragraph, and sentence level. Fast-pacing is an element in some genres such as thrillers, whereas slow pacing is an element in other genres such as epic fantasy.

Pantsing

1. The process of writing a novel without an outline ("flying by the seat of your pants")

See *Outlining*.

See also *Appendix B: Resources for More Learning* for useful resources on pantsing.

Pareto Principle

1. Principle outlined by economist Vilfredo Pareto that 80% of effects come from 20% of the causes (such as 80% of sales come from 20% of an author's books)

The Pareto Principle is so fundamental because you can see it in every aspect of the writing life. Usually, 20% of an author's books will drive 80% of their sales. Usually, 20% of an author's readers will send 80% of the fan mails.

However, the Pareto Principle is commonly mistaken as "you should spend 80% of your time doing X activity in order to get the best results," which is similar, but not the same.

Passive Income

1. Income derived from activities that do not require ongoing effort

Passive income activities usually involve creating content once and letting it work for you, such as releasing a video that promotes an affiliate link. In fact, affiliate income is one of the most lucrative passive income strategies because you can create a lot of content around certain products, and automate the traffic to them through ads.

As a personal aside, I make affiliate sales from videos I made YEARS ago.

Other examples of passive income include low-maintenance online courses, and of course, book sales, though one could argue that book sales are passive-aggressive—if you don't do something to market your books, they will eventually fall off the radar, but even if you do nothing, you'll still probably sell some.

See *Active Income*, *Cash Flow*, and *Income Stream*.

Pay-Per-Click Advertising

1. Advertising structure in which businesses bid for keyword search terms to appear high in search engine results; businesses pay every time a prospective customer clicks on the promoted link to their website or product

See *Click Rate*, *Conversion*, and *Impressions*.

Perfect Bound

1. Style of book binding in which a layer of adhesive on the book spine holds the pages together

Grab any paperback book off your bookshelf. Chances are that it's perfect bound. Print on-demand books are perfect bound too.

See *Binding*, *Print On-Demand*, and *Trade Paperback*.

Permafree

1. A book that is permanently free (a permafree book)

Authors may choose to make a book permafree as a loss leader to get the book into readers' hands in exchange for sales down the road. This is typically (and most effectively) done with Book 1 in a series.

See *Loss Leader*.

Piracy

1. The act of distributing copyrighted work without the legal permission to do so, usually via websites, torrents, and peer-to-peer file sharing applications

See *Copyright* and *Infringement*.

Platform

1. An audience of interested people around a cause
2. A social media website or tool an influencer uses to reach an audience

See *Influencer* and *Microinfluencer*.

Plot

1. The main events of a story in sequence

Plot Point Method

1. Plot structure popularized by Syd Field and Larry Brooks that outlines common bears (plot points) that occur in every story

See *Appendix B: Resources for More Learning.*

Podcast

1. A series of digital audio files made available to the public, usually via a free subscription

See *Blog* and *Vlog.*

Police Procedural

1. Mystery subgenre with a police or ex-police character that heavily emphasizes police procedure in solving crimes

See *Mystery.*

See also *Appendix C: Fiction Genres.*

Pomodoro Method

1. Time management method developed by Frances Cirillo in which one works at 25-minute increments with 5-minute breaks between

Pop-Up

1. An ad that disrupts the user's browsing experience by appearing on top of content

Many people consider pop-ups to be annoying, but as far as opt-ins are concerned, the conventional wisdom among marketers is that they work, and they work well.

See *Conversion*.

Portable Digital Format (PDF)

1. Digital file developed by Adobe that reliably reproduces text and images no matter what device it is viewed on

See *Ebook*, *Electronic Publication Format*, and *Mobipocket File*.

Portable Network Graphic File (PNG)

1. Highly quality, highly compressed digital image that can be downloaded quickly

Compared to a GIF or JPEG, the advantage of PNG files is that they tend to be smaller. PNG Files are also lossless, meaning they don't lose their quality when saved or altered. PNGs also support transparency better than JPEGs and GIFs.

See *Graphic Interface Exchange Format* and *Joint Photographic Experts Group File*.

Preface

1. Front matter element written by the author explaining the origin of the book

In case of confusion, a preface is similar to an introduction. It probably doesn't make sense to include both in a book, so pick the name that works best and use that.

See *Acknowledgments*, *Author's Note*, *Foreword*, *Front Matter*, and *Introduction*.

See also *Appendix A: Front and Back Matter*.

Press Kit

1. Kit that contains relevant marketing information
   about a business

Also known as a media kit. Businesses commonly host a press kit on their site that includes product specs, press releases, photos of product in different dimensions, and other interesting items that journalists can use to write feature articles about the product.

Authors can use press kits to feature themselves and their books to make it easy for a blogger or podcaster to cover their book.

See *Marketing.*

Price Anchoring

1. The act of using an initial price to influence a
   buyer's perceptions on the value of a product

Here's a great example of price anchoring: "I normally charge clients $99 for this course. But because I want you to be successful, and because it's Black Friday, I'm offering it for just $67."

By establishing the $99 price, everything that comes after will automatically sound cheaper.

Price anchoring is often a common tactic on sites with

tiered plans; the most popular plan will be highlighted to draw your eye to it. Once you see that first, you'll make automatic judgments about all the prices on the page.

Price-Matching

1. The act of one retailer matching another retailer's price for a given book, usually by algorithm

Amazon uses a price-matching to ensure that it has the best prices. For books, if it detects a lower price on another retailer such as Kobo, it will automatically drop the price of the book on Amazon to match the price.

Print On-Demand

1. The process of printing books as an author needs them, fulfilled and shipped by a printer

Print on-demand revolutionized the publishing industry and made self-publishing possible. Before print on-demand, if an author didn't want to be traditionally-published, they had no choice but to use vanity publishers, who used offset printing. The result was boxes upon boxes of books in the author's garage.

With print on-demand, authors don't have to pay upfront for a print run like they do with a printer. Instead, the book is printed and shipped when the author or customer asks for it.

. . .

See *Offset Printing*, *Trade Paperback*, and *Vanity Publisher*.

Print Run

1. In offset printing, a batch of books printed by a printer

See *Offset Printing* and *Print On-Demand*.

Prologue

1. In fiction, a front matter element that consists of a short chapter at the beginning of the novel that takes place before the story proper begins and sets the stakes for the story

See *Front Matter*.

See also *Appendix A: Front and Back Matter*.

Promotion

1. The process of selling a book to a target audience

Promotion involves buying ads, talking to anyone who might be interested in a book, doing podcast interviews and guest blogs, and many more active tasks.

See *Marketing*.

Proof

1. In printing, a test book printed by the printer provided to the author to check for any errors

Also known as a galley copy.

Proofreading

1. Type of editing in which an editor reviews a manuscript primarily for typographical errors; usually the last line of defense before publication

See *Developmental Editing*, *Copyediting*, *Editing*, and *Editor*.

Protagonist

1. The main character of a story

Also known as a hero or main character.

See *Antagonist*.

Pseudonym

1. A fictional name used by an author in publishing a book, for privacy, business, or personal reasons

An author may choose a pen name to protect the privacy of themselves or their family.

They may choose a pen name to keep their writing separate from another profession, such as the practice of law or real estate.

They may choose a pen name to distinguish a book from their other works because it's in a different genre and they don't want to confuse readers.

They may choose a pen name to circumvent a do not compete clause.

Or they may just choose a pen name because it sounds cool.

Public Domain

1. Collective body of work whose copyright has expired

Any work in the public domain can be freely used, shared, remixed, or altered for both personal and creative purposes.

If a work is not in the public domain, it cannot be used for any purpose without the copyright owner's consent.

See *Copyright* and *Creative Commons*.

Pulp Fiction (Era)

1. Period from approximately the 1900s to the 1950s in which commercial fiction short stories and novels were printed inexpensively in magazines ("pulps") and widely accessible to the public

The history of pulp fiction is long, fun, and far too interesting to delve into here. It is directly responsible for making commercial fiction into what it is today.

Pulp fiction has so many parallels to the self-publishing movement that it's worth studying. Indie authors are in many ways spiritual successors to pulp writers.

See *Appendix B: Resources for More Learning.*

Q

Query Letter

1. A letter written to a prospective literary agent that pitches the author's book and why the agent should read it

See *Book Proposal*, *Book Synopsis*, and *Literary Agent*.

R

Really Simple Syndication (RSS)

1. A web feed that allows a user to auto-download content whenever new installments are available, such as a podcast or blog

Most people have such busy lifestyles that don't have time to visit a blog every day, so instead, they download an RSS reader that aggregates all of their favorite blogs in one place. Same with podcasts.

See *Blog* and *Podcast*.

Recto

1. In a printed book, the right page

See *Verso*.

Regency Romance

1. Style of romance that takes place during the British Regency period (1811-1820), with a special set of reader expectations

Regency romance readers have very specific expectations. This is perhaps the most stylized and demanding romance genre. If an author does not follow those demands exactly, their book cannot be called a regency romance.

See *Historical Fiction*.

See also *Appendix C: Fiction Genres*.

Remainder

1. A book that does not sell and whose unsold copies are returned to the publisher and sold at a loss

See *Returns System*.

Repetitive Stress Injury (RSI)

1. An injury caused by repetitive movement (such as carpal tunnel)

This definition is included in this book for awareness. Many writers suffer from RSIs such as carpal tunnel. Having ergonomic equipment and healthy techniques is a must in this industry.

Resolution

1. The ending of a story

See *Climax, Denouement, Freytag's Pyramid.*

Returns System

1. System among publishers, distributors, and retailers
   that orchestrates how remaindered books are
   handled

The returns system is costly. Retailers generally won't purchase a book unless it can be returned. If a book doesn't sell, retailers can't sell the unsold copies, so they return them to the publisher at the publisher's expense. At this point, the publisher has lost their ability to make a profit so they must do whatever they can to recoup some costs by remaindering the books, which means selling them at a steeply discounted cost.

Often, remaindered books are destroyed.

This system can completely devastate an indie author, so it is best to avoid using this system when using offset printing unless you know what you're doing.

See *Remainder.*

Return on Investment (ROI)

1. Measure of how much money is being made for a product versus the amount of money invested

See *Margin*.

Reverse Harem

1. Genre in which a heroine is being courted by two or more men, on top of a regular narrative

Reverse Harem can be in any genre. It is a romance between a heroine and two or more men.

See *Appendix C: Fiction Genres*.

Review

1. A written opinion from a reader discussing what they liked or did not like about a book, usually located on a book's product page at an online retailer

Reviews are a critical marketing tool, as readers read them to decide what books to read. Virtually all book retailers allow readers to leave reviews.

Authors use the quantity and quality of reviews as social proof (such as a "four-and-a-half star average"). They may also use snippets from reviews to help sell their books.

As a general rule, it is never a good idea to pay for reviews. The review system is built on trust and integrity, and retailers, authors, and readers alike depend on this honest ecosystem. Violating this trust and integrity can be career-ending.

See *Advanced Reader Copy*, *Book Blog*, and *Street Team*.

Romance

1. Genre where the romance between two characters is at the forefront

See *Appendix C: Fiction Genres*.

Royalty

1. A sum paid to a copyright or patent holder by a licensee for use of the rights; for authors, this sum is a percentage of income from each copy of a book sold

Amazon and other online book retailers do not technically pay out "royalties", though they call them that. A royalty requires you to license your rights in exchange for a percentage of income for each book sold, and self-published authors do not license their rights to online book retailers when they publish on those platforms. Therefore, the accurate definition for online book retailer payments is "sales commissions."

See *Advance* and *Royalty-Free*.

Royalty-Free

1. Content that is purchased one-time without paying a royalty to the creator of the content

See *Copyright*, *Model Release* and *Royalty*.

Running Head (and Foot)

1. In a printed book, the header or footer of the book with the page number, author's name, title of the book, or chapter name

Running headers and footers can contain a number of different elements. There are certain rules on which pages running headers or footers should appear. Failing to follow these rules can make your book look amateurish.

S

Saddle-Stitching

1. Style of book binding in which the pages are held together by stitches or staples in the spine; common for poetry chapbooks

See *Binding* and *Chapbook*.

Sales Funnel

1. Series of steps that lead a customer from a less expensive (or free) product to a more expensive one

A proper sales funnel might look like this: an entrepreneur has a free podcast with great content that entices listeners to join their email list. When listeners join the email list, the entrepreneur sends an autoresponder sequence that promotes a cheap product (say $10). If the customer buys that product, after a certain amount of time they receive another autoresponder sequence that promotes a more expensive course, say $500. From the very beginning, the sales funnel is designed to lead them toward the course.

See *Conversion* and *Lead Magnet*.

Sales Rank

1. Position that represents how well a book is selling compared to all other books in an online retailer

Sans Serif Font

1. Font type without serifs

See *Font* and *Serif Font* for a full discussion of serif vs. sans serif fonts.

Science Fiction

1. Fiction genre in which science or scientific themes are at the heart of the story

Search Engine Optimization (SEO)

1. The process of using search engine best practices to improve a website's chance of ranking high in organic searches

See *Organic Search*.

Second Half Title

1. In some books with large front matter, a half title
   that appears at the end of the front matter, just
   before the body begins

See *Front Matter*, *Half Title*, and *Title Page*.

See also *Appendix A: Front and Back Matter*.

Secondary Rights

1. The right to resell a work after its first publication

See *First Rights*, *Foreign Rights*, *Subsidiary Rights*, *and World English Rights*.

Segmentation

1. In email marketing, the act of separating email
   subscribers into groups based on their engagement,
   demographics, actions they've taken in the past
   (such as buying a product), or some other important
   metric that is important to a business

Let's say that you have an email list of 1,000 subscribers, but you have a problem: no one seems to be opening your emails. So you segment the subscribers who haven't opened your email into a separate group so that you can email them one last time to try to reengage them.

Let's say that you have an email list with 10,000 subscribers, and you want to advertise your newest product only to those who bought your last book. You can segment those people into a separate list.

Segmentation is effective because you can view open and click rates for that group in isolation compared to your overall list, which may be helpful in many situations.

How segmentation works ultimately depends on the email service provider, but most providers allow you to do it some shape or form. It has many practical uses.

See *Autoresponder*.

Self-Editing

1. The process of an author editing their manuscript without the assistance of an editor

There are two types of self-editing. The first type is when an author self-edits their book as thoroughly as possible before sending it to an editor. The second type is when an author self-edits their manuscript without sending it to an editor. The second type is never a good idea.

. . .

See *Editing*.

Self-Publishing

1. The act of publishing a book without the assistance
    of a publisher

Also known as independent (or indie) publishing. Commonly
confused with *Vanity Publishing*.

See *Authorpreneur*, *Independent (Indie) Publisher*, and *Vanity Publisher*.

Sell Sheet

1. Document that provides information about a book,
    its availability and ordering methods

Also known as an advance information sheet (AIS).

See *Press Kit*.

Semi-Colon

1. A punctuation mark that indicates a connection
    between two clauses that could technically be
    standalone sentences

Semi-colons are often misunderstood; they are considered by many to be out of vogue. In fact, many authors actively choose not to use them.

However, they are useful in connecting two thoughts that could technically stand alone as complete sentences. The semi-colon connects them in a way that asks the reader to consider the relevance; if it weren't for the semi-colon, many readers might not pause to think about the connection.

For this reason, they're the punctuation of choice for essays (the nonfiction type, not the high school type). When used properly, they're a smart punctuation choice when you want to convey a stylized or sophisticated mood.

See *Colon*.

Sensitivity Reader

1. A paid reader who examines a manuscript for anything that might be offensive to readers (cultural, racial, sexual, etc.).

Sensitivity readers are a new trend. In today's society, which places ever more demands on everyone to be more politically correct (whether you agree with it or not), sensitivity readers claim to help authors navigate this by helping them fix anything that might be offensive, such as a Muslim character who uses magic.

Authors tend to fall into two schools when it comes to writing: they either write what they know or they don't. For the second school, there is always a risk that you will write something that may seem innocent to you, but offensive to someone of another race, like if you write a novel from the perspective of an Asian character but you're not Asian. There are some insights you just won't be able to have if you haven't lived in a culture different than yours.

That being said, I'm hesitant to recommend sensitivity readers because there's no true way to eliminate everything offensive from a book. No matter what you do, you're going to anger somebody. I argue that it actually might be better for an author to make a faux pas so that people engage them and it can be a learning experience.

See *Alpha Reader* and *Beta Reader*.

Serial

1. A narrative broken into regular installments, usually for television or radio

A soap opera is a classic example of a serial.

In the early days of self-publishing, authors used serials to great effect, writing and releasing parts (also known as episodes) several weeks apart, and then collecting them into "season" anthologies.

Readers like serials, but writing them poses some logistical challenges. How will you get each episode or part into readers' hands? Via email? Via a download? How will they download the book onto their reading device? Will you publish each part on book retailers? If you do, what do you do with the parts once the season is done? Do you take them down and lose your reviews, or do you keep them up and take the risk of them cannibalizing the sales of the bigger, more profitable season book? While there are answers to most of these questions, there is still no easy way to do serials without having some kind of logistical problem.

See *Series.*

Serial Comma

1. A comma used after the penultimate item in a list

Also known as an Oxford comma.

Let's say we have a list of items.
    Books.
    Pencils.
    Notebooks.
    If we use a serial comma, you would write them as books, pencils, and notebooks. You would place the serial comma after pencils.
    There is a lot of healthy debate among grammarians on the serial comma, but the common wisdom among most writers and editors is that you should use them.

·   ·   ·

See *Comma.*

Series

1. A group of related books in the same universe,
   usually meant to be read in sequential order

A series differs from a serial in that it is not released in short, easy to consume parts. In a series, full-length books are released rather than chapters or episodes.

See *Serial* for a longer discussion on serials. See also *Standalone Novel.*

Serif Font

1. Font type with serifs

Serifs are ornaments that appear on certain letters. Pick any novel off your bookshelf and pay very close attention to the letters (you can also use this book, which is printed in Fanwood, a serif font). Then go on any major website and look at the letters there.

The letters in a serif font almost always have embellishes, and slight strokes that seem to dig into the page, like on "g"s and "t"s. Look at the "g"s and "t"s on the website you chose and you will likely not see those embellishments.

Serif fonts are customary for printed books because they originate from handwriting and the early days of typesetting. They just look better on the printed page. Baskerville and Garamond are iconic serif fonts.

Sans serif fonts are better for digital reading and easier on the eyes because they are blockier. Arial and Helvetica are iconic sans serif fonts. Using a serif font on, say, a blog isn't completely forbidden, but it would have to be the right font or it might be difficult to read compared to what readers are used to.

Why does an author need to know about this, or even care?

Two reasons. First, I would make sure your paperbacks use serif fonts. It's the industry standard. Generally speaking, sans serif fonts in paperbacks make you look amateurish.

Second, depending on your genre, your book cover will make use of either one of these. Knowing whether your genre usually has a serif or sans serif font is a useful thing to know when you are providing instructions to your cover designer.

See *Font* and *Sans Serif Font*.

Shelf Life

1. The time an unsold book remains on the shelf of a bookstore before being removed

In the print world, all books have a shelf life. In the ebook world, a book has unlimited shelf life because it never goes out of stock unless the author or publisher unpublished it.

Short Story

1. Fully developed story that is shorter than a novel

See *Novel*.

Side-loading

1. The process of loading an ebook onto a reading
   device without the assistance of a retailer's
   ecosystem or delivery service

Side-loading is important because there are readers who prefer to own their ebooks, and they may purchase their books outside of a retailer like Amazon, and have a need to load the books onto their devices.

Readers who buy their books directly from authors often need to side-load their books onto their reading devices. With most devices, there are a number of steps you have to follow to download a book from a computer onto the device. There are programs that also can help with this task.

Of course, there are piracy concerns with side-loading, but that's beyond the topic of this definition.

Slush Pile

1. Collection of unread novel, short story, or poem

submissions awaiting a literary magazine editor's review

See *Unsolicited Manuscript*.

Small Caps

1. Lowercase-sized letters that are capitalized

See *Drop Caps*.

Small Press

1. A traditional publisher that is not a part of a large corporation and is usually smaller in size, has fewer sales, employees, books, and associates authors

See *Traditional Publisher*.

S.M.A.R.T Goal

1. Acronym for Specific, Measurable, Attainable, Realistic, and Timely; used to measure the efficacy of a goal

S.M.A.R.T goals are better goals. If I said "I want to write a book someday," it is not likely that I will ever do it.

If I said "I want to write a 50,000-word novel in 2 months with a deadline of January 31st," that's much better because it satisfies all of the S.M.A.R.T elements.

Smart Contract

1. Computer program that executes legally binding contracts

Smart contracts are automated and can facilitate, verify, or enforce digital agreements. As part of blockchain technology, they have the power to replace lawyers and banks in financial transactions.

See *Blockchain* and *Disintermediation*.

Smart Quotes

1. Curly quotation marks

Smart quotes are always preferable because they are more attractive to the eye. Most word processors have settings that will automatically change "straight quotes" to smart quotes.

Social Proof

1. External validation of a creator's content through public fan support, such as product reviews, number of followers, social media shares, etc. (both in quantity and quality)

Squeeze Page

1. On a website, a landing page intended solely to convince visitors to take an action, such as joining a mailing list

A good squeeze page has the following elements:

- A great headline that catches the viewer's attention
- Convincing sales copy
- No navigation or any other links. The viewer must take the action you want or leave the website.
- Pleasant images or video
- A call to action. Depending on what the action is, it may be repeated throughout the page. Most authors won't do this unless they are selling an informational product.

See *Call to Action*.

Space Opera

1. Subgenre of science fiction set in space, with space travel and space adventure as major themes

See *Science Fiction.*

See also *Appendix C: Fiction Genres.*

Split Test

1. The process of testing one or more versions of content to see which performs better

Also known as A/B testing.

Split testing is commonly done with email marketing, web advertising, copywriting, and anything that is customer-facing. The goal is to optimize an ad, image, or piece of content to its fullest potential so that it converts at the highest rate.

Common things authors can split test are book covers, book descriptions, and ads through Facebook or Amazon.

Split testing can be done manually or through specialized apps and services.

. . .

See *Conversion.*

Sponsorship

1. The act of a business paying for access to an influencer's audience (such as a sponsored video)

Standalone Novel

1. A novel whose story is fully concluded at the end of the book

Just because a novel is a standalone, it can still be part of a series. Many detective novels, for example, are standalone novels within a series.

See *Serial* and *Series.*

Steampunk

1. Fiction genre that takes place in a world (usually Victorian) where steam technology is the main source of technology

See *Appendix C: Fiction Genres.*

Stock Content

1. Photos, graphics, audio, and video that can be purchased royalty-free for use in a creator's content

See *Copyright, Model Release, Royalty-Free* and *Creative Commons.*

Street Team

1. Team of an author's dedicated readers who agree to read advance reader copies of the author's work, post early reviews, and promote an author's newest work upon release

See *Advanced Reader Copy* and *Review.*

Style Sheet

1. A document that outlines the proper nouns, stylistic preferences, and other elements that an editor can use to edit a work effectively

Style sheets make editors' lives easier. It tells them all of your proper nouns and the correct spellings so that they can correct any errors. It tells them grammatical preferences such as whether to use a serial comma, how to address numbers, and so much more.

Editors who work for traditional publishing houses usually edit according to a house style guide.

Subsidiary Rights

1. Rights beyond the ebook, paperback, and audio editions of a book, such as film, television, graphic novels, etc.

See *First Rights, Foreign Rights, Secondary Rights,* and *World English Rights.*

Sweet Romance

1. Style of romance novel that does not feature explicit sex

See *Erotica, Romance.*

See also *Appendix C: Fiction Genres.*

SWOT Analysis

1. Process a business can use to determine where they

fit in the marketplace and what their weaknesses are.

SWOT stands for strengths, weaknesses, opportunities, and threats. By analyzing all four elements, a business can develop a clear picture of where they stand and what they need to do to improve and defend against competitors.

T

Table of Contents (TOC)

1. Front matter element that lists all the chapters, sections, and elements in a book

For table of contents in ebooks, see *Navigational Control for XML*.

Target Audience

1. Group of people that are likely to be most interested in a business's product or service, based on their demographics, interests, internet activity, or history of buying similar products or services

See *Niche*.

Terms of Service

1. Contract that governs how a website or product can be used, what is expected of all parties to the contract, and what happens if one party breaches the contract

Almost no one reads terms of service, and it's a shame, because many of them are scary.

My grandfather always liked to say that if you ever knew what went into a hotdog, you would never eat one again. If you ever knew what attorneys put in terms of service, you might think twice about signing one again.

Let me tell you a story about my own stupidity and why I always advocate to read the terms of service for any website or product that you use.

I once purchased gum online. This was a special kind of gum, designed to be stronger, longer lasting, and dentist-approved. I don't have any medical problems; I just saw an ad one day on the Internet and thought it looked cool.

And let me tell you, the gum was phenomenal. It tasted great, lasted a long time, and it was so cheap that I signed up for a subscription, which is where everything went wrong.

The company sent me so much gum that I honestly did not need a subscription. It was enough to last me months. So I went online and tried to cancel my subscription, except there was no place for me to do that. In fact, there was no cancel button anywhere on the website. So I read the terms of service, and it said to cancel a subscription, you just had to email the customer service team.

I sent them an email. No response.

So I sent another one.

No response.

I called the phone number listed in the terms of service. It was disconnected.

Eleven emails later, my subscription renewed against my consent and I found myself in a very difficult situation. I had to notify the consumer protection bureau in the state where they did business, which was an exercise in frustration. I ultimately had to file a fraudulent charge with my credit card company, which was a hassle. And to make matters worse, I got another box of gum.

I read the rest of the terms, and to my horror, parts of it were incomplete. From what I could tell, the company basically took a template from somewhere and slapped it on their website without bothering to customize it.

If it weren't for a personal connection I had that happened to put me in touch with someone at this company, I would have been in some real trouble.

I made my life complicated, all because of a box of gum.

Let this be a lesson to always read the terms of service, even if it's for a stick of gum. If you sense even something slightly wrong, walk away and don't agree to it.

Always read any contract you sign, and read it with scrutiny.

Terms of service are by definition boilerplate contracts. You cannot customize them. You must agree or not use the service.

See *Boilerplate Language*.

Termination and Reversion of Rights Clause

1. In a publishing contract, a clause that states what happens if one party fails to uphold their obligations, and what happens to the author's copyright as a result

If a publisher goes bankrupt, what happens to an author's copyright? What if a conglomerate acquires the publisher? What if a book just isn't selling and the author wants the rights back so they can self-publish? What if the publisher fails to publish the book in the first place, or if the author decides not to provide the manuscript or doesn't agree with the editing, or virtually any other scenario that could go wrong?

The termination and reversion of rights clause address that. As a general rule, every termination and reversion clause is different. One of your many goals in a rights negotiation should be to get reversion of rights as quickly as possible. In the early days of self-publishing, there were many stories of traditionally-published writers whose books weren't selling and the authors wanted the rights back but couldn't get them because of contracts they signed decades ago. Don't let that happen to you.

See *Grant of License* and *License*.

See also *Appendix D: Copyright*.

Three-Act Structure

1. Plot structure that takes place in three separate acts that signify a beginning, middle, and end; common in plays

See *Appendix B: Resources for More Learning*.

Title Page

1. Front matter element with the title of the book, author name, and if applicable, the publisher

See *Front Matter*, *Half Title*, and *Second Half Title*.

See also *Appendix A: Front and Back Matter*.

Trademark

1. A symbol, slogan, or image that distinguishes a company or product in the marketplace, and that is legally registered with the government

The Coca-Cola logo is a trademark, as is the slogan "Share a Coke." Whenever they appear, these things help consumers know that they are looking at a Coca-Cola product. Should another soda company try to co-opt Coca-Cola's logo or slogan, Coke could sue because any infringement could create customer confusion.

Most authors are unlikely to ever file a trademark for their books, but they do need to beware of using certain trademarks in their book, either by mentioning them or using images with them. Some businesses like to control their brand very tightly and don't want consumers to think even for a moment that their product could be affiliated with a business they don't approve of.

When in doubt, genericize any products in your books.

Instead of Xerox, say copy machine.

See *Copyright*, *Infringement*, and *Trade Dress*.

Trade Dress

1. The visual appearance or characteristics of a
   product that distinguishes it in the marketplace,
   registered with the government

Coca-Cola's bottle is a classic example of trade dress. Its slim
shape is iconic and defines the brand.

The green and yellow color palette of John Deere products
distinguish them in the market place. Woe be to any tractor
company that tries to rip this off.

See *Trademark*.

Trade Paperback

1. A softcover paperback that is typically sturdier,
   larger, and better quality than a mass market
   paperback

Also known as a softcover. Trade paperbacks are what authors
refer to when they mean "paperbacks." They are used in offset
printing and print on-demand.

. . .

See *Mass Market Paperback*, *Print On-Demand*, and *Trim Size*.

Trade Publishing

1. The field of publishing that produces books in the most popular genres such as fiction and nonfiction

Trade publishing is exactly what you think it is. All genres of fiction and nonfiction are included.

Textbooks, research papers, and other highly specialized reference books are not considered to be trade books.

Also known as legacy publishing (derogatory).

See *Traditional Publisher*.

Traditional Publisher

1. A publisher who publishes an author and pays them royalties in exchange for an assignment of copyright

See *Acquisitions Board*, *Big Five Publishers*, *Imprint*, *Small Press*, and *Trade Publishing*.

Transcription

1. The act of migrating an audio file to the written
    word, either by hand or by computer software

See *Dictation* and *Optical Character Recognition (OCR)*.

Trim Size

1. The height and width of a physical book

Some of the most common self-published paperback trim sizes
are 6 x 9, 5 x 8, 5.25 x 8, and 5.5 x 8.5.

See *Mass Market Paperback* and *Trade Paperback*.

Troll

1. One who actively and publicly degrades an author
    and their work

Every author has critics and haters. Trolls take it to the next
level by making personal attacks on the author and by
spreading lies or private information about the author, all in an
attempt to intimidate the author or get a visible response.

Some trolls even make death threats. It goes without saying that this type of behavior should never be tolerated and any trolling comments should always be eliminated from your website or social media. However, to engage trolls is exactly what they want. It's far better to ignore them and let their public behavior stand as a testament to their lack of character.

Trope

1. A motif shared by all fiction

Other definitions of tropes exist, but they are, for the most part, beyond the scope of this book and apply mainly to speech and rhetoric.

The most common way tropes are used in author language is for recurring themes in fiction, such as a hero with "short man" syndrome, a power-hungry prince, or a pot-smoking hippie. These are all archetypes that you can see in any story, and each of them carries a certain connotation and assumption about what they are. These "mental" assumptions are shaped by culture and every creative endeavor that has ever existed and become part of society's collective conscious.

Some motifs appear in certain genres more frequently, such as vampires who are vulnerable to sunlight in urban fantasy, or spaceships that are falling apart but that are beloved by their owner in space opera.

The concept of "writing to market" is based on the idea that if you use the tropes that readers expect, then your book will sell. That's not really true, but it hasn't stopped authors from chasing tropes to try to make money.

Tropes are not good or bad; they just are. It's how you use

them that counts.

See *Writing to Market.*

See also *Appendix E: Writing to Market.*

Typography

1. The style and appearance of written words,
    typically on a visual medium like a book cover

See *Cover* and *Font.*

U

Unsolicited Manuscript

1. A submitted manuscript not requested by an agent, editor, or publisher

Some literary agents, magazines, and publishing houses do not accept unsolicited manuscripts.

See *Slush Pile*.

Upsell

1. The act of promoting upgrades or add-ons to a customer at the point of sale to increase profits

"Would you like to Super-Size your fries and drink?"

That's a line formerly used at McDonald's to upgrade customers from regular-sized fries and sodas to gigantic ones that defined fast food restaurant portion sizes for decades. It's a classic upsell, perhaps one of the most famous of all time.

"Would you like to add the extended warranty for your computer for an additional twenty dollars?"

You get the picture.

Upselling differs from cross-selling in that the goal is to improve or complement the products that the customer is already buying. With cross-selling, you're selling them another product entirely.

. . .

See *Bundling* and *Cross-Sell*.

Urban Fantasy

1. Subgenre of fantasy that generally takes place in an urban environment with supernatural creatures, and magic

See *Appendix C: Fiction Genres.*

V

Value-Added Tax (VAT)

1. A tax imposed on goods sold in the European Union

Tax laws are ever-changing and outside the scope of this book, but the gist of the VAT is that if a customer who lives in the European Union buys your book, book retailers have to tax them a certain percentage depending on what country they live in. The tax is in addition to the sale price and generally subtracted from an author's royalties.

Where authors have to be careful is if they are doing direct sales to customers in the EU because they may be required to collect the VAT tax if their third-party payment platform does not.

Vanity Publisher

1. A publisher who charges a fee to an author in exchange for publication

Back in the bad old days, self-publishing was synonymous with vanity publishing. If you couldn't get a traditional publishing contract, you could hire a vanity publisher for thousands of dollars to produce an inferior product and have boxes upon boxes of books in your garage. Under this model, it was assumed that the author published the books for their "own vanity," hence the name.

In general, vanity publishers should be avoided. However, there are reputable companies who do provide fair and ethical publishing services to writers without appealing to their "vanity", and whose pricing is far more reasonable. Michael La Ronn's personal opinion is to publish by yourself, but in some cases that may not be appropriate due to personal circumstances. If you feel that this path is for you, I recommend that you check The Alliance of Independent Authors' Watchdog Desk for reviews they've done on publishing companies to discover which companies to engage and which ones to avoid.

Vanity publishing is also known as a form of partnership publishing (or shared publishing), in which an author and publisher both share the cost of the book's production. Partnership publishing is sometimes used as a euphemism for vanity publishing, but is not always considered the same.

See *Assisted Self-Publisher*, *Hybrid Publisher*, *Print On-Demand*, and *Self-Publishing*.

Verso

1. In a printed book, the left page

See *Recto*.

Vlog

1. A blog in video format

Originally known as a video weblog (archaic).

See *Blog* and *Podcast*.

Virtual Assistant (VA)

1. A remote worker who helps a business with the day-to-day tasks of running an author's business

Of course, assistants can be hired locally, but they're significantly more expensive due to health insurance, taxes, and workers compensation (in the United States at least). You also have to provide a space for that person to work, usually.

Virtual assistants can be hired on a per task basis or on a salary. Depending on your needs, they can be employees on your payroll or independent contractors.

They can assist with just about anything, from email screening to light proofreading to video editing.

See *Authorpreneur*.

Webinar

1. A video training session conducted over the
   Internet, usually with a call to action at the end

Many Internet entrepreneurs have turned webinars into
money-making machines, offering trainings and then selling a
product such as a digital course for more advanced learning.

Western

1. Fiction genre that takes place in the North
   American West in the late 19th and 20th centuries,
   usually featuring cowboy heroes

See *Appendix C: Fiction Genres.*

Wholesale Pricing Model

1. Sales model where the book publisher sets a
   recommended price of the book, but the retailer
   can discount the price in order to sell it

Under the wholesale pricing model, publishers set the price of
books and sell them to retailers at a discount. The retailer then

sells the book at a price where they can make a profit. This is how traditional publishing operates today.

On another front, Amazon engages in discount pricing for print books. Let's say that a publisher lists a print book there. The publisher lists the book for $14.99, but Amazon discounts the book to $12.99 in order to sell more copies. The author would receive a royalty based on the $12.99 price point.

See *Agency Pricing Model*.

Work for Hire

1. In the United States, a doctrine that an employer owns the copyright to creative work created by an employee in the course and scope of their employment

Work for hire can be a complex area of copyright law. Freelancers, ghostwriters, and virtual assistants also commonly run into it.

See *Copyright, Freelancing, Ghostwriting*.

See also *Appendix D: Copyright*.

World English Rights

1. In a publishing contract, a license for the publisher

to publish certain formats of a book in every
country in the world that speaks English

See *First Rights*, *Foreign Rights*, *Grant of License*, *License*, *Secondary Rights*, and *Subsidiary Rights*.

Writing to Market

1. In fiction, the process of writing saleable
commercial fiction by appealing to what readers
want

See *Appendix E: Writing to Market*.

Writing into the Dark

1. Writing process popularized by Dean Wesley Smith
in which you write a book without an outline,
explained in his book *Writing into the Dark*

Y

Young Adult (YA)

1. Fiction genre that features mid-to-late teenage protagonists coming of age, usually targeted at readers age 12-18 and up

See *Middle Grade*, and *New Adult*.

See also *Appendix C: Fiction Genres*.

Next Steps

I hope you found *The Indie Writer's Encyclopedia* useful. If you did, here is how you can get more writing advice from me.

* Subscribe to my YouTube channel, Author Level Up. I publish videos every week with in-depth writing advice.

* And lastly, join my Author Level Up newsletter, where you'll get free tips and notifications whenever I launch a new book or an important video.

Let's keep in touch. I wish you all the best in your writing career.

Peace, love, and light,

. . .

M.L. Ronn

Read Next: How to Write Your First Novel

Are you still dreaming about writing that book?!

Learning how to write your first novel can be overwhelming. You have to master outlining, writing, revising, and so much more...and it can be scary if you've never done it before.

While it seems daunting, writing your first novel is simple when you have someone experienced to help you through it.

In this writer's guide, prolific writer M.L. Ronn shares an easy step-by-step process of writing compelling fiction that he's perfected after writing 40+ books.

Write your first novel with structured advice tailored for beginners:

- Learn the basic building blocks of every story and how to put them together
- Develop an effective outline (or learn how to write without one!)
- Discover winning formulas that mega-bestsellers use to write their novels
- Navigate your novel's "murky middle" with 7 unorthodox strategies that will get you unstuck in no time
- Revise your story without fear

Writing your first novel is life-changing. Download this writer's guide, follow the step-by-step instructions, and you'll wake up one morning very soon with a finished manuscript waiting for you.

Purchase How to Write Your First Novel today by visiting www.authorlevelup.com/firstnovel.

Meet M.L. Ronn

Science fiction and fantasy on the wild side!

M.L. Ronn (Michael La Ronn) is the author of many science fiction and fantasy novels including *The Good Necromancer*, *Android X*, and *The Last Dragon Lord* series.

In 2012, a life-threatening illness made him realize that storytelling was his #1 passion. He's devoted his life to writing ever since, making up whatever story makes him fall out of his chair laughing the hardest. Every day.

Learn more about Michael
www.authorlevelup.com (for writers)
www.michaellaronn.com (fiction)

More Books by M.L. Ronn

Books for Writers

Indie Author Confidential (Series)
    How to Write Your First Novel
    Be a Writing Machine
    Mental Models for Writers
    The Indie Writer's Encyclopedia
    The Indie Author Atlas
    The Indie Author Bestiary
    The Reader's Bill of Rights
    The Self-Publishing Compendium
    150 Self-Publishing Questions Answered
    Authors, Steal This Book
    The Indie Author Strategy Guide
    The Author Editing Problem
    Interactive Fiction: How to Engage Readers and Push the Boundaries of Story Telling
    Indie Poet Rock Star
    Indie Poet Formatting

2016 Indie Author State of the Union

Fiction (as M.L. McKnight)

The Good Necromancer (Urban Fantasy)
Shadow Deal
Cold Hard Magic
Spirit Chaser

The Chicago Rat Shifter (Urban Fantasy)
Dead Rat Walking
Rat City

Fiction (as Michael La Ronn)

Magic Trackers (Urban Fantasy)
Dream Born
Nightmare Stalkers
Evil Waking

Modern Necromancy (Urban Fantasy)
Death Marked
Death Bound
Death Crowned

Standalone Urban Fantasy
Magic Souls: An Interactive Urban Fantasy

The Last Dragon Lord (Dark Fantasy)
Old Dark
Old Evil
Old Wicked

Sword Bear Chronicles (Fantasy Adventure)
Theo and the Festival of Shadows

Galaxy Mavericks (Space Opera)
Honor's Reserve
Phantom Planet
Zero Magnitude
Garbage Star
Solar Storm
Rogue Colony
Orbital Decay
Planet Eaters
Horizon Down

Moderation Online (Gamelit)
Food City
Salad Days
Delicious Zeal

Android X (Sci-Fi Adventure)
Android Paradox
Android Deception
Android Winter

Short Story Collections
Reconciled People
The Expanding Universe Vol. 3

Poetry (as Elliott Parker)
Muse Poems
Android Poems

Nonfiction:

www.authorlevelup.com/books

Fiction:

www.michaellaronn.com/books

Appendix A: Front and Back Matter

Front and back matter has a long, storied order that publishers have used for a long time. According to Joel Friedlander in his book *The Book Blueprint: Expert Advice for Creating Industry-Standard Print Books*, the proper order of front and back matter elements is as follows:

Half title
    Frontispiece
    Title page
    Copyright page
    Dedication
    Epigraph
    Table of contents
    List of figures
    List of tables
    Foreword
    Preface
    Acknowledgments
    Introduction

Prologue
Second half title
Body
Part opening page
Chapter opening page
Epilogue
Afterword
Conclusion
Postscript
Appendix or addendum
Chronology
Notes
Glossary
Bibliography
List of contributors
Index
Errata
Colophon

Of course, no book will have all of these elements, but this list is a good resource to use when you need to know what order everything should be in.

Resources for Further Learning

The Book Blueprint: Expert Advice for Creating Industry-Standard Print Books by Joel Friendlander.

Appendix B: Resources for More Learning

The following is a massive book list to help you explore all the topics I covered in the book further. This isn't an exhaustive list by any means, but it's enough to give you functional knowledge in virtually every area of publishing.

If you'd like, feel free to go shopping using my Amazon affiliate link: www.authorlevelup.com/goshopping. I'll receive a small commission on whatever books you buy. If you find this list helpful in anyway, it's an easy way to say thanks, and if you do, thank you!

Business

How to Make a Living as a Writer by James Scott Bell

The Write Way: Everything You Need to Know About Publishing, Selling, and Marketing Your Book by Amy Collins

Six-Figure Author: Using Data to Sell Books by Chris Fox

. . .

The Business of Being a Writer by Jane Friedman

Business for Authors: How to Be an Author Entrepreneur by Joanna Penn

How to Make a Living With Your Writing by Joanna Penn

The Successful Author Mindset: A Handbook For Surviving the Writer's Journey by Joanna Penn

Creating Your Author Brand by Kristine Kathryn Rusch

The Freelancer's Survival Guide by Kristine Kathryn Rusch

How Authors Sell Publishing Rights by Helen Sedwick and Orna Ross

Killing the Sacred Cows of Publishing (Series) by Dean Wesley Smith

Intellectual Property

The Copyright Wars: Three Centuries of Trans-Atlantic Battle by Peter Baldwin

. . .

The Copyright Handbook: What Every Writer Needs to Know by Stephen Fishman

Marketing & Promotion

Start Marketing Your Book: Best Practices & Core Principles for Authors Selling Books Online by Ella Barnard

No Plot? No Problem! A Low-Stress, High-Velocity Guide to Writing a Novel in 30 Days by Chris Baty

How to Write a Sizzling Synopsis: a Step-by-Step System for Enticing New Readers, Selling More Fiction, and Making Your Books Sound Good by Bryan Cohen

Help! My Facebook Ads Suck: Simple ways to turn those ads around by Michael Cooper

Pep Talks for Writers: 52 Insights and Actions to Boost Your Creativity by Grant Faulkner

Ads for Authors Who Hate Math by Chris Fox

Write to Market, Launch to Market, and Relaunch Your Novel by Chris Fox

.   .   .

Let's Get Digital: How to Self-Publishing and Why You Should by David Gaughran

Strangers to Superfans: A Marketing Guide to the Reader Journey by David Gaughran

Gotta Read It! Five Simple Steps to a Fiction Pitch That Sells by Libbie Hawker

Get Your Book Selling: Jumpstart Your Sales With a Simple Plan That Just Works by Monica Leonelle

Mastering Amazon Ads: An Author's Guide by Brian Meeks

Mastering Amazon Descriptions: An Author's Guide by Brian Meeks

How to Market a Book by Joanna Penn

Discoverability: Help Readers Find You in Today's World of Publishing by Kristine Kathryn Rusch

Reader Magnets: Build Your Author Platform and Sell More Books on Kindle by Nick Stephenson

.   .   .

The Adweek Copywriting Handbook: The Ultimate Guide to Writing Powerful Advertising and Marketing Copy from One of America's Top Copywriters by Joseph Sugarman

Writing a Better Book Description: Capture More Readers and Sell More Books by Kevin Tumlinson

Miscellaneous Resources

Cover Design Secrets You Can Use to Sell More Books by Derek Murphy

Ready to be a Thought Leader? How to increase your influence, impact and success by Denise Brousseau

Public Speaking for Authors, Creatives, and Other Introverts by Joanna Penn

The Healthy Writer: Reduce your pain, improve your health, and build a writing career for the long term by Joanna Penn and Dr. Euan Lawson

Productivity

The Writer's Guide to Training Your Dragon: Mastering Speech Recognition Software to Dictate Your Book and Supercharge Your Writing Workflow by Scott Baker

. . .

Dictate Your Book: How to Write Your Book Faster, Better, and Smarter by Monica Leonelle

Be a Writing Machine: Writer Smarter, Beat Writer's Block, and Be Prolific by M.L. Ronn

The Creativist Compendium by Orna Ross

The Pursuit of Perfection and How It Harms Writers by Kristine Kathryn Rusch

Writing with Chronic Illness: Improve Outlook and Productivity by Kristine Kathryn Rusch

The Part-Time Artist: Stay Creative and Pay Your Bills by Céline Terranova

Get It Done: Hard-Hitting Motivation for Authors by Jonathan Yanez

Publishing Contracts

Getting to Yes: Negotiating Agreement Without Giving In by Roger Fisher, William L. Ury, and Bruce Patton

Closing the Deal on Your Terms: Agents, Contracts, and Other Considerations by Kristine Kathryn Rusch

.   .   .

How to Negotiate Anything: A Freelancer's Survival Guide Short Book by Kristine Kathryn Rusch

The Self-Publisher's Legal Handbook by Helen Sedwick

Playing the Short Game by Douglas Smith (for short stories)

How Authors Sell Publishing Rights by The Alliance of Independent Authors

Writing, Outlining & Editing

How to Write Pulp Fiction by James Scott Bell

Write Your Novel from the Middle by James Scott Bell

Story Engineering: Mastering the 6 Core Competencies of Successful Writing by Larry Brooks

Story Physics: Harnessing the Underlying Forces of Storytelling by Larry Brooks

Self-Editing for Fiction Writers: How to edit yourself into print by Renni Browne and Dave King

Writing Active Hooks (Series) by Mary Buckham

. . .

Plotto: The Master Book of All Plots by William Wallace Cook

Heroes & Heroines: Sixteen Master Archetypes by Tami D. Cowden, Caro LaFever, and Sue Viders

Fallen Heroes: Sixteen Master Villain Archetypes by Tami D. Cowden

GMC: Goal, Motivation & Conflict by Debra Dixon

2k to 10K: Writing Faster, Writing Better, and Writing More of What You Love by Rachel Aaron

5000 Words Per Hour: Write Faster, Writer Smarter by Chris Fox

Take Off Your Pants! Outline Your Book for Faster, Better Writing by Libbie Hawker

On Writing: A Memoir of the Craft by Stephen King

Write Better, Faster: How to Triple Your Writing Speed and Write Every Day by Monica Leonelle

Become a Successful Indie Author by Craig Martelle

. . .

How to Write Non-Fiction by Joanna Penn

Write. Publish. Repeat. The No-Luck-Required Guide to Self-Publishing Success by Sean Platt and Johnny B. Truant

Iterate and Optimize: Optimize Your Creative Business for Profit by Sean Platt and Johnny B. Truant

The One With All the Writing Advice by Sean Platt and Johnny B. Truant

How to Write Your First Novel: The Stress-Free Guide to Writing Fiction for Beginners by M.L. Ronn

Writing Habit Mastery: How to Write 2,000 words a Day and Forever Cure Writer's Block by S.J. Scott

Heinlein's Rules: Five Simple Business Rules for Writing by Dean Wesley Smith

Writing into the Dark: Write a Novel Without an Outline by Dean Wesley Smith

. . .

The McGraw-Hill Desk Reference for Editors, Writers, and Proofreaders by K.D. Sullivanand Merilee Eggleston

Creating Characters: How to Build Story People by Dwight V. Swain

Techniques of the Selling Writer by Dwight V. Swain

Outlining Your Novel: Map Your Way to Success by K.M. Weiland

Structuring Your Novel: Essential Keys for Writing an Outstanding Story by K.M. Weiland

Specialized Books for Writing in Certain Subject Areas

Maim Your Characters (Series) by Samantha Keel (how to write injuries realistically)

Indie Poet Rock Star (Series) by Michael La Ronn (how to self-publish poetry)

Throwing Lead: A Writer's Guide to Firearms (and the People Who Use Them) by J. Daniel Sawyer and Mary Mason

A Civilian's Guide to the U.S. Military: A Comprehensive Reference to the Customs, Language, & Structure of the Armed Forces by Barbara Schading

. . .

Closest to the Fire: A Writer's Guide to Law and Lawyers by Karen A. Wyle

YouTube Videos on Author Level Up

I've put together a playlist for you that contains the following videos mentioned in this book:

- Buying a Writing App: 10 Tips
- How to Write an Engaging Character: 26 Tips
- How to Outline a Novel in 10 Ways
- Types of Fantasy Novels
- Types of Sci-Fi Novels

Watch the playlist at http://www.authorlevelup.com/encyclopediavideos

The Alliance of Independent Authors

Become a Member: http://www.authorlevelup.com/alli

Watchdog Desk: https://selfpublishingadvice.org/self-publishing-service-reviews/

Appendix C: Fiction Genres

Here is a list of subgenres for all the major fiction genres. This isn't an exhaustive list, but it's enough to get you started: www.authorlevelup.com/fictiongenres

Appendix D: Copyright

Books

The Copyright Wars by Peter Baldwin

The Copyright Handbook by Stephen Fishman

How Authors Sell Publishing Rights by Helen Sedwick and Orna Ross

The Self-Publisher's Legal Handbook by Helen Sedwick

Online Resources

Entertainment Law Update Podcast with Gordon Firemark: https://entertainmentlawupdate.com/

· · ·

CrashCourse Guide to Intellectual Property [YouTube Series]: http://www.authorlevelup.com/crashcourseip

CopyrightX Lectures by William Fisher (52 lecture course on copyright law taught by a leading attorney & expert, all free on YouTube): http://www.authorlevelup.com/copyrightxlectures

Creative Commons: http://www.creativecommons.org

Plagiarism Today: https://www.plagiarismtoday.com/

Appendix E: Writing to Market

Books

Write to Market by Chris Fox

Tropes

TVTropes: http://www.tvtropes.org

Courses

Write to Market without Selling Your Soul by Michael La Ronn: http://www.authorlevelup.com/writetomarket

Index of Terms by Category

Business

Design

Cover
> Font
> Monospaced Font
> Sans Serif Font
> Serif Font
> Typography

Editing

Alpha Reader
> Beta Reader
> Chicago Manual of Style
> Colon
> Comma
> Copyediting
> Developmental Editing
> Editing
> Editor
> Ellipsis
> Em Dash
> En Dash
> Fleisch-Kincaid Score
> Fragment
> Proofreading
> Self-Editing
> Semi-Colon
> Sensitivity Reader
> Serial Comma
> Style Sheet

Ebook and Paperback Formatting

Alignment
Bleed
Drop Caps
Electronic Publication Format (ePUB)
Gutter
Interior
Justification
Mobipocket File (MOBI)
Navigational Control for XML (NCX)
Running Head (and Foot)
Small Caps
Smart Quotes

Elements of a Book

About Page
Acknowledgments
Appendix
Author's Note
Back Matter
Bibliography
Binding
Body
Casewrap
Chapbook
Chapter
Chronology
Colophon
Conclusion
Copyright Page
Cover Spread
Dedication

Dust Jacket
Endnotes
Epigraph
Epilogue
Folio
Foreword
Frontispiece
Front Matter
Glossary
Half Title
Index
Introduction
Novel
Perfect Bound
Preface
Prologue
Proof
Recto
Saddle-Stitching
Second Half Title
Table of Contents
Title Page
Trim Size
Verso

Fiction Genres

Cozy Mystery
Cyberpunk
Erotica
Fantasy
Historical Fiction
Horror
LitRPG

Fiction Writing

Legal

Lead Magnet
Loss Leader
Mailing List
Marketing
Microinfluencer
Niche
Non-Disclosure Agreement (NDA)
Open Rate
Opt-In
Opt-Out
Organic Search
Pay-Per-Click Advertising
Permafree
Platform
Pop-Up
Press Kit
Price Anchoring
Price-Matching
Promotion
Review
Sales Funnel
Sales Rank
Segmentation
Social Proof
Split Test
Squeeze Page
Sponsorship
Street Team
Target Audience
Upsell

Productivity

Publishing Industry Terms

First Rights
Foreign Rights
Frontlist
Ghostwriting
Go Direct
Go Wide
Hybrid Author
Hybrid Publisher
Imprint
Independent Bookstore
Independent (Indie) Publisher
International Standard Book Number (ISBN)
Kindle
Kindle Unlimited
Kindle Direct Publishing (KDP) Select
List Price
Literary Agent
Mass Market Paperback
Master of Fine Arts (MFA)
Midlist
Midlist Author
National Novel Writing Month (NaNoWriMo)
Narrator
Offset Printing
Out-of-Print
Print On-Demand
Print Run
Pseudonym
Pulp Fiction (Era)
Query Letter
Remainder
Returns System
Secondary Rights
Self-Publishing

Technology

Joint Photographic Experts Group File (JPEG)
Markdown
Metadata
Native Content
Optical Character Recognition (OCR)
Podcast
Portable Digital File Format (PDF)
Portable Network Graphic File (PNG)
Really Simple Syndication (RSS)
Search Engine Optimization (SEO)
Side-loading
Smart Contract
Transcription
Vlog